Treatment of Error in Second Language Student Writing

Treatment of Error in Second Language Student Writing

Dana R. Ferris

California State University, Sacramento

 Michigan Series on Teaching Multilingual Writers

Ann Arbor

THE UNIVERSITY OF MICHIGAN PRESS

Copyright © by the University of Michigan 2002
All rights reserved
Published in the United States of America by
The University of Michigan Press
Manufactured in the United States of America
♾ Printed on acid-free paper

2005   2004   2003   2002   4   3   2   1

A CIP catalog record for this book is available from the British Library.

Library of Congress Cataloging-in-Publication Data

Ferris, Dana.
    Treatment of error in second language student writing / Dana R.
Ferris.
        p.   cm. — (Michigan series on teaching multilingual writers)
    Includes bibliographical references.
    ISBN 0-472-08816-5 (cloth : acid-free paper)
    1.   English language—Study and teaching—Foreign speakers. 2.
English language—Rhetoric—Study and teaching. 3.   Report writing—
Study and teaching. 4.   English language—Errors of usage. 5.
Second language acquisition. I.   Title. II. Series.
PE1128.A2 F474   2002
808′.042′071—dc21   2001006442

For Randy, Laura, and Melissa

Contents

How can ESL writing teachers use their time wisely and avoid burnout in giving error feedback?

5. Beyond Error Correction: Teaching Grammar and Self-Editing Strategies to L2 Student Writers   77

Raising student awareness about the importance of accuracy and self-editing

Teaching editing strategies

Providing instruction through grammar minilessons (including specific recommendations about available texts and materials)

Holding students accountable and helping them to track progress

Appendixes

Series Foreword

Error treatment is one of the key second language (L2) writing issues faced by classroom teachers, teacher trainers, and teacher researchers. No matter how ideologically wary of grammar instruction we might be, a commitment to helping multilingual writers—whether in a class specifically for ESL/EFL students, first-year composition, or any other context in which writing is required—makes it difficult to avoid grappling with the error-response issue at some level. Dana R. Ferris's willingness and ability to tackle this controversial and challenging topic are amply demonstrated in this concise, user-friendly, theory-into-practice book, one of the first volumes in the *Michigan Series on Teaching Multilingual Writers*.

Drawing on her admirable blend of researcher/classroom-practitioner experience, Ferris provides what many of us have long been looking for: a highly accessible and principled approach to both the theory and practice of error treatment that can guide pedagogical decision making. Unlike a teacher's manual or a handbook that purports to give all the answers needed, Ferris's research-based volume offers a solid scholarly foundation for the practical ideas presented together with an abundance of illustrative sample texts. This book will likely be seen as a rich resource in language-teaching methodology courses, but experienced teachers too will no doubt benefit from the depth and breadth of Ferris's coverage of various error-response techniques as well as of the research that motivates those techniques.

Perhaps what is most remarkable about this volume is Ferris's theory- and practice-informed challenge to simplistic and at times pessimistic notions of error treatment in L2 writing. Ferris offers a realistic, well-reasoned account of what L2 writing teachers, or any teachers of L2 students, need to know about error and how to put what they know to use. She persuasively addresses the fundamental error-treatment questions that plague novice and expert writing specialists alike: What types of errors should we respond to? When should we respond to them? What are the most efficacious ways of responding to them? And ultimately, what role should error treatment play in the teaching of the process of writing?

We are delighted to be able to make Dr. Ferris's work available through the *Michigan Series on Teaching Multilingual Writers*.

Diane Belcher, Ohio State University
Jun Liu, University of Arizona

Preface

     My own interest in the treatment of error in second language (L2) student writing began, literally, in various women's restrooms on several university campuses in the latter half of the 1980s. This was where I and other ESL teachers would talk about a dilemma that we all struggled with. We had been trained to be "process-approach" writing teachers (following seminal works such as Zamel 1982 and Krashen 1984)—encouraging multiple drafting, revision, collaboration, and an emphasis on ideas, with attention to language issues (grammar, vocabulary, spelling, punctuation, and other mechanics) being intentionally postponed to the very end of the composing process. What this often meant, in practice, was that grammar and editing issues were almost never addressed by teachers or their students in the ESL writing classroom. And yet, we found, the students' language problems were not magically disappearing as the sure result of a more enlightened process and view of writing. Worse, L2 writers themselves, painfully aware of their own linguistic deficits and the need for teacher intervention, were disappointed with instructional policies such as "I will not correct your journal entries, your freewrites, or your early essay drafts. You should be focusing on expressing your ideas and building fluency and not worrying about grammar until 'later.'"

This simultaneous awareness of persistent written error and of student frustration led to whispered restroom discussions.

"I'm teaching grammar in my writing class."

"I am, too. I *have* to. They *need* it!"

To those of us trained in process philosophies and techniques, error correction, grammar instruction, and editing-strategy training felt like the "dirty little secrets" of our writing classes. We were ashamed because we felt that we should "know better" and that we and our students should have "moved beyond" these issues. Still, our sense of what students needed overrode these considerations, and the treatment of error continued, albeit somewhat underground.

My own need to understand what might help my university ESL writers to improve the linguistic accuracy of their texts has led me over the past ten years to pursue a variety of classroom research projects (see, e.g., Ferris 1995c, 1997; Ferris et al. 1997; Ferris and Roberts 2001) and to develop teaching materials for ESL writing classes and for teacher preparation courses. This book pulls together the results of these explorations in what I hope is a coherent and holistic approach to the treatment of error in L2 writing classes.

I would be remiss if I did not acknowledge the contributions of others to my own thinking on this topic. First and foremost, I must thank the hundreds of ESL writers and MA TESOL graduate students in classes at California State University, Sacramento, from 1990 to the present, who have served as willing guinea pigs for my research efforts and as test pilots for my teaching materials. I am also grateful to the many ESL teachers in our program at CSUS who have generously cooperated in data-collection efforts over the years and have utilized my materials. In particular, I want to thank Sarah Chaney, Shelagh Nugent, Gabriella Nuttall, Barrie Roberts, and Stuart Schulz, all of whom taught in the Learning Skills Center at CSUS and allowed me and others to collect data in their classrooms; thanks also go to Professors Robby Ching and Sue McKee of the Learning Skills Center. My colleagues in the MA TESOL Program in the English Department at CSUS, Linda Callis Buckley, Marie Helt, and Fred Marshall, have been instrumental in shaping my thinking about grammar issues and especially about teacher preparation options. I am also grateful to CSUS for providing me with various grants of release time and funding that have enabled me to carry out many of these projects and to the English Department (especially the former and current chairs, Ted Hornback and Mark Hennelly) for allowing me to accept these grants.

I must also acknowledge my former graduate students, now professional colleagues, who worked with me on research projects over the years: Sarah Chaney, Rich Harroun, Hiliry Harvey, Tina Jordan, Keiko Komura, Gabriella Nuttall, Susan Pezone, Christiana Rennie, Barrie Roberts, Cathy Tade, and Sharee Tinti. I am further indebted to many other colleagues in the field, including Pat Byrd, Jan Frodesen, John Hedgcock, Janet Lane, Genevieve Patthey-Chavez, Charlene Polio, Joy Reid, and Tony Silva, who have read my manuscripts and discussed grammar and editing issues with me over the years. I am particularly grateful for the support of series editors Diane Belcher and Jun Liu, who paid me the compliment of approaching me with this book project and who have been tremendously supportive and encouraging as I have worked on it. And as always, I am thankful for the ongoing advice and support I receive from Professor Robert Kaplan, formerly my Ph.D. advisor and now a trusted mentor.

Finally, my heartfelt appreciation goes to my husband, Randy Ferris, and my daughters, Laura and Melissa Ferris, for their encouragement and their patience.

Introduction

Treatment of Error in Second Language Student Writing provides an in-depth discussion of the treatment of error in L2 writing classes, including a synthesis of previous research on error correction in writing courses and extensive practical applications and advice for teachers of L2 writers. More than an isolated list of suggestions for "error correction" or "teaching grammar to student writers," the volume approaches the *treatment of students' written error* in a comprehensive and integrated way that assumes that such treatment involves not only teacher feedback and grammar instruction but also consciousness raising, strategy training, and student accountability. In addition, present and future writing instructors will find in this volume information not only about how to teach students but about what teachers need to know to adequately treat written error.

Books on L2 writing have typically been extremely theoretical and research oriented or, when they are of a more practical nature, limited by space considerations in their treatment of specific pedagogical topics. For instance, my own coauthored teacher training text (Ferris and Hedgcock 1998) is highly practical, but as it includes nine individual topics, it is hard for any one issue to be covered with the depth and detail practicing teachers need. There is just one chapter on grammar, editing, and error-correction issues. A book that thoroughly connects theory and practice on this vital issue should fill a great need for ESL writing teachers.

This book contains an up-to-date overview of the theoretical issues and research findings related to error correction and the teaching of grammar to L2 student writers (chaps. 1–2). The majority of the book, however, is devoted to providing specific, concrete, practical information for in-service and preservice teachers of L2 writers. The ultimate goal of the book is that both new and experienced teachers, using the resources provided in the book, could:

- adequately prepare themselves to respond to grammar errors and provide instruction;
- accurately assess students' needs for error correction and grammar instruction;
- provide written feedback on student papers that not only helps students to "fix" problems in current texts but will lead to long-term improvement in accuracy and writing style;
- teach minilessons that help writers to grasp key terms and rules needed for writing and to develop effective strategies for editing their own work both out of class and under time pressure.

Each chapter includes illustrations and lists of specific suggestions. In addition, samples of student writing and teachers' error markings are included as appendixes. Sample exercises for both ESL writing students and preservice ESL writing instructors are included as well.

Chapter 1

Why Is Error Treatment Necessary for L2 Writers?

Over the short but eventful history of teaching composition to L2 writers, teachers' and theorists' views of the importance of grammar, error correction, and accuracy have undergone several shifts. Writing for L2 students was, until the 1970s, primarily perceived as language practice, designed to help students manipulate grammatical forms or utilize newly learned vocabulary items (Ferris and Hedgcock 1998; Johns 1990; Raimes 1991; Silva 1990). Writing in L2 classes typically consisted of "controlled" or "guided" composition activities in which students, for instance, would write a paragraph about "what I did yesterday" in order to practice the use of the past tense or would change the nouns in an already constructed paragraph from singular to plural forms. Because of the influence of behavioral psychology and structural linguistics on second language teaching, teachers gave a great deal of attention to students' accuracy or lack thereof, constantly correcting all errors so that no bad habits would form. In addition, teachers carefully taught students grammatical forms and rules assumed to be problematic because of contrasts with students' native languages. Thus, error correction and grammar instruction were major, perhaps even the primary, components of writing instruction in L2 classes.

In the 1970s, native-English-speaking composition practitioners and theorists began to focus on writers themselves and on the processes they used to construct texts. This led to a major paradigm shift that had great implications for both L1 and L2 writing classes in the United States. Rather than emphasizing correct forms for essays, paragraphs, and sentences, teachers and students were encouraged to focus on discovering ideas, drafting, revising, working collaboratively, and sharing successes. Though process-approach advocates gave lip service to the continued importance of accuracy in students' finished products, attention to grammar was left to the end of the process (or the "editing" phase). Generally, it was assumed that if students were engaged in writing about topics they had chosen themselves and were empowered to make decisions about the shaping and polishing of their own texts, final products would improve as a natural consequence of a more enlightened process. Since both teachers and students found it more stimulating and less tedious to focus on ideas than on accuracy, composition instruction entered a period of "benign neglect" of errors and grammar teaching.

As process pedagogy entered L2 writing classes, some scholars almost immediately began to express concerns about the neglect of accuracy issues and its effects on ESL writers. An early piece entitled "Meanwhile, Back in the Real World . . ." (Eskey 1983) reminded us that the ability to correct errors is crucial in many settings and that students' accuracy will not magically improve all by itself. Similar concerns were raised by Horowitz (1986), who also pointed out the limitations of the process approach for teaching ESL writers to function in real academic settings. Other scholars began to note the inherent differences between L1 and L2 writers and to suggest that pedagogical suggestions designed for native speakers needed to be critically reevaluated in light of these distinctions (e.g., Leki 1990; Silva 1988, 1993; Zhang 1995). One of the inescapable differences between L1 and L2 student writers is that the nonnative speakers make errors related both to negative transfer from their L1s and to incomplete acquisition of the L2. Though L1 student writing is obviously not error free, the errors made are different in quantity and nature. Because L2 students, in addition to being developing writers, are still in the process of acquiring the L2 lexicon and morphological and syntactic systems, they need distinct and additional intervention from their writing teachers to make up these deficits and develop strategies for finding, correcting, and avoiding errors.

Second Language Acquisition and Its Implications for Error Correction

As most L2 teachers and learners are only too aware, second language acquisition (SLA) takes time and occurs in stages. Though SLA research is not conclusive as to specific orders and stages of acquisition, several generalizations have emerged.

- It takes a significant amount of time to acquire an L2, and even more when the learner is attempting to use the language for academic purposes.
- Depending on learner characteristics, most notably age of first exposure to the L2, some acquirers may never attain nativelike control of various aspects of the L2.
- SLA occurs in stages. Vocabulary, morphology, phonology, and syntax may all represent separately occurring stages of acquisition.
- As learners go through various stages of acquisition of different elements of the L2, they will make errors reflective of their SLA processes. These errors may be caused by inappropriate transference of L1 patterns and/or by incomplete knowledge of the L2. Written errors made by adult L2 acquirers are therefore often quite different from those made by native speakers.

These insights from SLA research have several practical implications for teachers of L2 writers. First, it is unrealistic to expect that L2 writers' production will be error free or that, even when it is, it will "sound" like that of native English speakers. Second, since SLA takes time, we should not expect students' accuracy to improve overnight. Third, and most important for the purposes of this book, L2 student writers need: (a) a focus on different linguistic issues or error patterns than native speakers do; (b) feedback or error correction that is tailored to their linguistic knowledge and experience; and (c) instruction that is sensitive to their unique linguistic deficits and needs for strategy training.

The remaining chapters of this volume will focus on these

pedagogical issues. Chapters 2 and 3 address the types of errors L2 writers most typically make and how those are distinct from the error patterns of native-English-speaking student writers as well as what L2 writing teachers need to know about grammar in order to address their students' particular needs. Chapter 4 looks in detail at error feedback and how teachers can most effectively communicate with students about their errors. Chapter 5 deals with the types of grammar and editing instruction that will most benefit ESL writers.

Objections to Error Correction in L2 Writing Classes

As already noted, the advent of the process approach in L1 and L2 writing instruction in the 1970s and 1980s led to a decreased focus on student error. Since then, a number of scholars have questioned the appropriateness of this trend, some conservatively noting that L2 writers may be distinct enough from L1 writers to merit different pedagogical strategies (e.g., Leki 1990; Nelson and Carson 1998; Silva 1993; Zhang 1995) and others taking stronger stances, arguing that noninterventionist teacher strategies have been "cruelly unfair to diverse students" (Johns 1995, 182) or have produced adults with years of U.S. English education, even at the college/university level, who cannot function in either academic or workplace settings (Scarcella 1996). The resulting renewed interest in error correction, grammar instruction, and editing-strategy training for L2 student writers can be observed in the publication of "how-to" articles and books for teachers (e.g., Bates, Lane, and Lange 1993; Ferris 1995c; Ferris and Hedgcock 1998; Frodesen 1991; Reid 1998b) as well as editing handbooks for ESL student writers (e.g., Ascher 1993; Fox 1992; Lane and Lange 1999; Raimes 1992) and chapters in mainstream composition textbooks on ESL editing issues.

In addition, a number of researchers over the past ten years have examined the effects of error correction and/or editing instruction on student revision and improvement in accuracy (e.g., Fathman and Whalley 1990; Ferris 1995a, 1997; Polio, Fleck, and Leder 1998).

Despite—or perhaps because of—this renewed interest in grammar for ESL writers, an article published in *Language Learning* in 1996 by John Truscott argues for the abolishment of grammar correction in L2 writing classes. Truscott claims that there is no convincing research evidence that error correction ever helps student writers, that error correction as typically practiced overlooks SLA insights about how different aspects of language are acquired, and that practical problems related to teachers' and students' ability and willingness to give and receive error correction make it a futile endeavor. He concludes that error correction is not only useless to student writers but that it is actually harmful in that it diverts time and energy away from more productive aspects of writing instruction. Truscott's review essay, published in one of the leading L2 journals, has aroused a good deal of debate both in conference presentations and in published work to date (Ellis 1998; Ferris 1999a; Ferris and Hedgcock 1998; Truscott 1999).

In my own response to Truscott (Ferris 1999a), I argue that his conclusions are premature, primarily because the body of research evidence he cites is inadequate and inconsistent in its methodology and subject characteristics, and that further research on error correction is necessary before final recommendations can be made to ESL writing teachers. While it may be fair to say that "those who claim editing instruction or corrective feedback is useful have the burden of demonstrating such effectiveness" (Polio, Fleck, and Leder 1998, 60), there are nonetheless several compelling reasons for teachers not only to continue the practice of giving error feedback and providing editing-strategy training but to seek ways to improve the effectiveness of these practices.

The first reason is that several research studies (including Polio, Fleck, and Leder 1998) have demonstrated that error feedback can help students to improve their accuracy in the short term, in other words, on revisions of the same essay or on targeted patterns of error over the course of a semester (Fathman and Whalley 1990; Ferris 1995c, 1997; Lalande 1982).

In a recently completed study (Ferris et al. 2000), it was found that 92 ESL student writers were able to successfully correct errors during revision after receiving teacher feedback. Of over 5,700 errors marked and coded, nearly 85 percent of them were corrected effectively by students during revision. Truscott (1996) and Polio, Fleck, and Leder (1998) correctly point out that there is little evidence that error feedback helps students improve their accuracy over the long term and that if students do show improvement, this may possibly be attributed to other factors such as additional writing practice and exposure to the L2. Indeed, it is challenging to measure long-term improvement in students' written accuracy and to attribute such development, if found, solely to teacher feedback. Nonetheless, it certainly may be argued that long-term development is unlikely without observable short-term improvement, at least in the ability to attend to and correct errors when pointed out by teachers. Thus, this small but growing research base, while it does not answer all theoretical questions related to error correction, should not be ignored as meaningless, either.

Second, as noted by a number of researchers, students value teacher feedback on their errors and think that it helps them to improve their writing (Cohen 1987; Cohen and Cavalcanti 1990; Ferris 1995b; Ferris et al. 2000; Ferris and Roberts 2001; Leki 1991; Radecki and Swales 1988). Truscott anticipates this argument and responds that "students believe in correction . . . but that does not mean that teachers should give it to them" (1996, 359) and that teachers should, rather than giving into this student desire, help students adjust to the absence of grammar correction. However, given the unquestioned (even by Truscott) strength of student demand for error correction, the possible harm to student motivation and confidence in their instructors may far outweigh any possible "damage" that could come to them from providing error feedback. Most ESL writing instructors know that were they to refuse to give any error feedback or grammar instruction, it would cause a great rift between them and their students. This potential negative outcome is not one that may be dismissed lightly or overcome easily (Brice and Newman 2000).

Finally, instructors need to work at finding the best ways to help their students become "independent self-editors" of their own work (Bates, Lane, and Lange 1993; Ferris 1995c). This is because accuracy is important in the real world to which student writers go. Both anecdotal and research evidence suggests that at least in some settings, university professors and employers find ESL errors distracting and stigmatizing (Hendrickson 1980; Janopolous 1992; Santos 1988; Scarcella 1996; Vann, Lorenz, and Meyer 1991; Vann, Meyer, and Lorenz 1984). Student writers' lexical, morphological, and syntactic accuracy is important because a lack of accuracy may both interfere with the comprehensibility of their message (or ideas) and mark them as inadequate users of the language. Writing instructors surely have some responsibility to arm their students with the knowledge, strategies, and resources they will need to function effectively outside of the ESL writing classroom. Though research may still be inconclusive as to the best ways to accomplish these goals, it seems clear that if L2 writing teachers abdicate this responsibility altogether, students are unlikely to make progress in editing skills and overall accuracy.

Thus, while it is important to acknowledge that the research database on error correction and grammar instruction is incomplete (as it is in many, if not most, areas of ESL teaching!) and that scholars have raised objections to the practice of error correction in ESL writing classes, this book proceeds on the assumption that most teachers—and certainly their students!—nonetheless believe in the potential for error correction, grammar instruction, and editing-strategy training to have positive effects on student writers' overall development. The remainder of this book is devoted, therefore, to identifying ways in which teachers can prepare themselves and their students to focus on accuracy in writing most effectively.

Chapter 2

Perspectives on Error Correction in L2 Writing

As has been demonstrated, there is disagreement and even controversy among L2 writing specialists and SLA theorists as to the nature and very existence of "error" and as to whether any classroom intervention, such as teacher feedback and formal grammar instruction, can help students to improve in written accuracy over time (Corder 1971; Ferris 1999a; James 1998; Reid 1998b; Truscott 1996, 1999). The purpose of this chapter, therefore, is to look at this debate more carefully by attempting to synthesize and critically analyze the various strands of research available on the topic of error treatment for L2 student writers. It concludes by summarizing what we know at this point—examining on what questions we have inadequate evidence and on what issues there is no concrete evidence to speak of at all—and by outlining a possible classroom research agenda for L2 writing teachers and scholars.

This examination of the debate responds to several key questions and their related subpoints, which are outlined in figure 1.

1. What are the effects of teacher error correction on student writing?

Adequacy of Teacher Feedback

In discussing the effects of teacher error correction, it is first necessary to address a charge that has been leveled by several researchers and reviewers: That a major reason why studies

1. *What are the effects of teacher error correction on student writing?*
   - Do writing teachers give accurate and complete feedback on students' errors?
   - Do students attend to teacher feedback and attempt to utilize it in revisions of their texts?
   - Do students who receive teacher feedback on their errors make accurate changes in their revisions?
   - Do students who receive error feedback improve in written accuracy over time?
   - Does it matter what types of feedback students receive (e.g., direct or indirect, coded or uncoded)?
   - Are certain types of error more "treatable" by means of error feedback than others?

2. *What are the effects of other types of classroom intervention on the accuracy of student writing?*
   - Does required revision after receiving feedback facilitate student progress?
   - Does in-class grammar instruction help students to improve their writing?
   - Does maintenance of error logs or charts help students to become more accurate over time?

3. *What are students' views and perceptions about error treatment in their writing?*
   - Do L2 student writers value error feedback, or do they resent it and find it discouraging and demotivating?
   - Do students value feedback on errors as much as feedback on other aspects of writing (e.g., ideas, organization)?
   - What specific feedback styles or mechanisms do students prefer (e.g., selective or comprehensive, direct or indirect)?

4. *What research questions need to be further explored?*
   - What parameters and issues need to be considered and controlled for?
   - What questions need additional investigation?
   - What new questions need to be addressed?

Fig. 1. Issues and questions to be reviewed

have failed to show positive effects for error correction on student accuracy is that the feedback given by teachers is incomplete, idiosyncratic, erratic, and inaccurate (Cohen and Cavalcanti 1990; Cohen and Robbins 1976; Truscott 1996; Zamel 1985). Cohen and Cavalcanti conducted a case-study analysis in which they analyzed the feedback given by one teacher to three students—a high performer, an intermediate performer, and a low performer—in each of three distinct settings (three teachers and nine student writers in total). While they did not examine the accuracy of teacher error correction, they do note that the different teachers "only dealt with approximately half the issues that could have been dealt with" or "avoided or overlooked over twice as many problems as [they] commented on" (1990, 160–61). In other words, the teachers' feedback was not comprehensive: it did not address all of the language issues independently identified by the researchers.[1] However, the authors also note that their design did not include a means to assess whether such omissions were "a conscious choice . . . an oversight, or the result of lack of knowledge about that issue" (1990, 173) and suggest that a "Teacher's Checklist" could be added to better address this question.

Cohen and Robbins (1976) followed the progress of three ESL college students over a semester, examining a variety of student texts, to assess (among other things) whether teacher error correction appeared to influence student progress in accuracy over time. They report that "the corrections did not seem to have any significant effect on student errors. But a closer look at the whole correction process suggested that the specific process of correction was at fault, rather than correction in general" (1976, 50). In particular, corrections were given at various times by three different instructors (the main instructor and two volunteer aides), leading to a possible lack of consistency. While it certainly seems possible and even likely that having three different instructors, two of whom were "volunteer aides," may have led to inconsistent or faulty error correction, no data are presented in support of this claim.

Unlike the two small-scale case studies by Cohen and his co-authors, Zamel's (1985) study of teacher commentary on student writing considers a more substantial sample of subjects—15 teachers, each responding to three or more students, on a total of 105 ESL student papers, not including revisions (85).

In a now-famous and often-cited quote, Zamel reports that "ESL writing teachers misread student texts, are inconsistent in their reactions, make arbitrary corrections, write contradictory comments . . . [and] overwhelmingly view themselves as language teachers rather than writing teachers; they attend primarily to surface features of writing. . . . " (1985, 86). Unfortunately, though Zamel goes on in the article to provide numerous clear examples and illustrations of her claims about teacher feedback, she does not provide any information about her method of analysis nor any statistics to indicate whether the examples she provides are truly representative of the entire sample of 105 student papers responded to by 15 different writing instructors. As in the case of Cohen and Robbins's (1976) study, while the assertions made by the author seem believable, they are not well supported by actual data (at least not as reported in the article).

In a recently completed study, Ferris et al. (2000) examined both the accuracy and completeness of error feedback given by three university ESL teachers to 92 ESL writers. In all, 146 texts and 5,707 errors marked by teachers were analyzed. It was found that the error corrections made by the teachers were correct in about 89 percent of the instances, with 3.6 percent judged as "incorrect" and 7 percent judged as "unnecessary." In a separate analysis of 110 unmarked papers from the sample, it was found that the teachers marked over 83 percent of the errors identified independently by two researchers.[2] In sum, while it may well be true that some L2 writing instructors are inaccurate and inconsistent in providing error feedback, there are as yet no studies that support this claim empirically and one that refutes this charge.

Student Uptake of Error Feedback

Another criticism of teacher error correction and of written feedback in general that has been advanced is that students do not pay attention to it, either for revision or for future writing projects (Cohen 1987; Truscott 1996). Few studies of error correction have examined this issue directly by looking at preliminary student drafts and teacher feedback and then tracing the changes potentially attributable to that feedback in subsequent student writing. In one such study (Fathman and Whalley 1990), the method of analysis included only overall scores of "content" and "grammar" quality on initial drafts and revisions, and there was no mechanism for assessing student uptake of particular teacher comments and corrections. In an experimental study by Frantzen and Rissell (1987), 22 students in a university Spanish class were given 10 minutes to correct errors that had been marked by the instructor/researcher, with "an incentive of a slightly improved grade given to those who corrected at least 75 percent of their corrected errors" (93). The subjects successfully corrected nearly 92 percent of all of the errors marked; however, it is not clear whether the remaining 8 percent of the errors were ignored by the students or whether they attempted corrections judged unsuccessful. Further, a controlled experimental situation in which direct incentives are given for editing may not illustrate what students might do with teacher corrections under more naturalistic circumstances. In a study of 1,467 teacher comments on 110 pairs of student papers, Ferris (1997) found that of 109 comments made specifically about grammar issues, only 15 (14 percent) were not addressed by the students in their revisions. Finally, in the study by Ferris et al. (2000), it was found that of 5,707 errors marked by teachers, students attempted corrections in 90.7 percent of the cases. (Of the errors, 9.3 percent were coded "no change," meaning that the identical error reappeared in the student revision.) Though the evidence on the question of whether students attend to teacher feedback is admittedly very limited, it is important to note that student survey research has consistently found that students claim to highly value teacher feedback on their grammar problems (see the discussion later in this chapter). Assuming these student self-reports are at least somewhat accurate, it would seem likely that L2 student writers would act on teacher error feedback in most cases.

The Influence of Error Feedback
on Student Revision

A related question is whether students make correct revisions on papers in response to teacher feedback. The evidence on this question that exists to this point is fairly conclusive: Though there is variation across error types, individual students, and teacher feedback mechanisms, student writers have generally been successful in producing more accurate revisions in response to error feedback. As already mentioned, the subjects in Frantzen and Rissell's (1987) study were able to self-correct nearly 92 percent of the errors marked by the teacher. In Fathman and Whalley's (1990) study, 100 percent of the students who received grammar feedback received higher grammar scores on their revisions (184, table 2). In Ferris's (1997) study, 73 percent of the grammar-focused teacher comments led to successful changes in the student revisions— notable because these were verbal comments made in the margins or in end notes, as opposed to at the point of error in the text.[3] In the study by Ferris et al. (2000), students made successful edits of about 80 percent of the errors marked by their teachers. Finally, in a recent study by Ferris and Roberts (2001), 53 university ESL writers who received error feedback were able to self-correct 60 to 64 percent of the errors marked during a 20-minute in-class editing session.

The Long-Term Effects of Error Feedback
on Student Accuracy

While it is interesting to observe whether students attend to and successfully incorporate teacher error feedback into papers they immediately revise, it is arguably more important to assess whether such intervention actually helps students to acquire correct language forms and improve their self-editing strategies, as measured through improved written accuracy over time. One of Truscott's (1996) major criticisms of the existing body of research on error correction in L2 writing is that there is little evidence that teacher feedback facilitates improvement of student writing in the long run. While Truscott is certainly correct that sustained improvement in writing quality is more important than editing texts from one draft to the next, a couple of qualifications are necessary. First, it can be very difficult to demonstrate conclusively, using longitudinal designs, that error feedback helps students to improve the overall quality of their writing. Researchers face a "catch-22" of sorts: If they show that feedback can be tied to short-term editing success, using controlled experimental designs (as in Fathman and Whalley 1990; Ferris and Roberts 2001; Frantzen and Rissell 1987), reviewers immediately observe that such findings say nothing about long-term student progress. On the other hand, if naturalistic longitudinal designs are utilized, critics note that, rather than improvement being attributable to teacher feedback, other intervening factors—increased writing practice, exposure to English inside and outside the classroom, etc.—may have led to students' progress. Secondly, it also could be argued that short-term improvement is necessary for longer-term progress. Thus, rather than seeing students' success in self-editing revisions as irrelevant to long-term improvement in accuracy and overall writing quality, it could be argued that such editing activities are necessary steps along that road.

That said, studies that assess students' progress in written accuracy over time generally do demonstrate that those who receive error feedback show measurable, often statistically significant, improvement. However, it is important to mention that only six studies to date have actually compared students who received error feedback with those who received no error feedback (Ashwell 2000; Fathman and Whalley 1990; Ferris and Roberts 2001; Kepner 1991; Polio, Fleck, and Leder 1998; Semke 1984)—and that of those, only the latter three used longitudinal designs. Of those three studies, Kepner's (1991) study shows an advantage in accuracy for the students who received error correction; Polio, Fleck, and Leder's (1998) study shows no difference between the feedback and no-feedback groups; and Semke's (1984) findings are inconclusive from the data reported. It is also important to note that the three studies varied from one another on just about every research parameter imaginable—subject characteristics, duration of treatment, types of student texts and teacher feedback being considered, and analysis methods. Thus, the question of whether there are quality differences between "the writing of students who have received grammar correction over a period of time [and] that of students who have not" (Truscott 1996, 329) is one that is clearly and critically in need of much more research.

However, there is a body of research work that examines the progress of students over time in written accuracy when they receive error feedback. Rather than contrasting subjects directly with groups of students who received no feedback, these studies compare students' test scores and/or written texts for grammar knowledge and accuracy at the beginning and end of treatment (typically the duration of a writing course, e.g., a quarter or a semester). Absent a true control group that received no error feedback at all, it is difficult to claim that any observed student improvement can be attributed solely or even primarily to teacher feedback (Truscott 1996). On the other hand, if Truscott is correct that error feedback is ineffective and even harmful to student writing, we might expect to see either no progress or even regression (i.e., less accurate writing) in the texts of students who received error correction from teachers over a period of time.

In reality, the studies that measure student progress in accuracy are rather consistent in showing that students who received error feedback reduced their overall ratios of errors over time (Chandler 2000; Ferris 1995a, 1997; Ferris et al. 2000; Frantzen 1995[4]; Lalande 1982; Polio, Fleck, and Leder 1998[5]; Robb, Ross, and Shortreed 1986; Sheppard 1992). The only study that does not demonstrate student progress in accuracy is the three-subject case study by Cohen and Robbins (1976). As already noted, the authors themselves suggest that this lack of progress may have been due to ineffective feedback strategies, especially because feedback was delivered at various points by three different individuals, two of whom were volunteer classroom aides. Again, without true control groups in these

Research Question	Studies Addressing the Question
Do students who receive error feedback produce more accurate writing in the short or long term than those who receive no error feedback?	Fathman and Whalley 1990; Ferris and Roberts 2001; Kepner 1991; Polio, Fleck, and Leder 1998; Semke 1984
Do students who receive error feedback show measurable improvements in accuracy over time?	Chandler 2000; Cohen and Robbins 1976; Ferris 1995a, 1997; Ferris et al. 2000; Frantzen 1995; Lalande 1982; Polio, Fleck, and Leder 1998; Robb, Ross, and Shortreed 1987; Sheppard 1992

Fig. 2. Studies of error feedback

studies, it cannot be conclusively argued that error correction caused the student improvement, which may have also resulted from other, uncontrolled variables such as instruction, increased writing practice, or even simply exposure to the L2 in and out of the classroom. However, the fact that the research shows consistent progress—not regression and not status quo—by students who received error feedback at least suggests that the correction may have helped them to improve. Figure 2 summarizes studies on the short- and long-term effects of teacher error correction on the accuracy of student writing.

Types of Feedback Mechanisms

As noted by Truscott (1996, 1999), most researchers and teachers appear to act on the presumption that error correction is helpful to students and focus instead on trying to identify the most effective mechanisms and strategies for giving error feedback. Thus, many studies of error correction in writing examine the effects of varying types of feedback on student accuracy. The most important dichotomy discussed in the literature is between direct and indirect feedback (Bates, Lane, and Lange 1993; Ferris 1995a, 1995c; Ferris and Hedgcock

1998; Hendrickson 1978, 1980; Lalande 1982). When an instructor provides the correct linguistic form for students (word, morpheme, phrase, rewritten sentence, deleted word[s] or morpheme[s]), this is referred to as **direct feedback.** If students are revising or rewriting their papers after receiving teacher feedback, they are expected merely to transcribe the teacher's suggested corrections into their texts. **Indirect feedback,** on the other hand, occurs when the teacher indicates that an error has been made but leaves it to the student writer to solve the problem and correct the error. It has been argued that indirect feedback is more helpful to student writers in most cases because it leads to greater cognitive engagement, reflection, and "guided learning and problem-solving" (Lalande 1982; see also Bates, Lane, and Lange 1993; Ferris 1995c; Ferris and Hedgcock 1998; Reid 1998b). Possible exceptions might include instances in which the error in question is complex and idiosyncratic (Chaney 1999; Ferris 1999a; Ferris and Roberts 2001) or when student writers are not sufficiently advanced in L2 proficiency to self-correct errors even when pointed out to them (Brown 1994; Ferris and Hedgcock 1998; Frodesen 1991).

Error-correction research to date points clearly to the overall long-term superiority of indirect feedback. In longitudinal studies by Lalande (1982), Frantzen (1995), and Ferris et al. (2000), groups of students who received indirect feedback significantly outperformed those who received direct feedback— in fact, in all three studies, the students receiving direct feedback either made no progress at all or even regressed in some error categories. On the other hand, Robb, Ross, and Shortreed (1986), who compared one group of students receiving direct feedback with three groups that received indirect feedback at differing levels of explicitness, report no significant differences across the four treatment groups, although all four groups showed improvement in accuracy. Still, since direct feedback is easier for students to utilize in their revisions, it could be argued that even a study that shows the indirect-feedback groups as equal to the direct-feedback group provides evidence in favor of indirect feedback.[6]

The study by Ferris et al. (2000) is unique in that it looks at the effects of different feedback treatments both in the short term (from one draft of a paper to the next) and in the long run (from the beginning to the end of the semester). Not surprisingly, it was found that in the short term, direct feedback led to more correct revisions (88 percent) than indirect feedback (77 percent). However, over the course of the semester, students who received primarily indirect feedback reduced their error-frequency ratios substantially more than the students who received mostly direct feedback. Again, because direct feedback is easier for students to act upon and requires less knowledge and effort on their part, it is not surprising that from one draft of a paper to the next it would show more positive effects than indirect correction. Nonetheless, as in Lalande's (1982) and Frantzen's (1995) studies, the cumulative effect of the differing treatments appeared to be that students who received indirect feedback improved in accuracy far more than those who did not.

Explicitness of Feedback

If indirect feedback is the superior choice in most cases, a follow-up question is how explicit such feedback needs to be. Several studies have examined the effects of **coded feedback** (in which the type of error, such as "verb tense" or "spelling," is indicated) versus **uncoded feedback** (in which the instructor circles or underlines an error but leaves it to the student writer to diagnose and solve the problem). Though survey research indicates that students and instructors feel that more explicit (i.e., coded) feedback is preferable and even necessary (Ferris et al. 2000; Ferris and Roberts 2001; Komura 1999; Rennie 2000; Roberts 1999), the text-analytic evidence that exists on this question does not support their intuitions. As previously noted, Robb, Ross, and Shortreed's (1986) study showed that there were no significant differences in student accuracy across three different types of indirect feedback (coded, underlined, and checkmarks in the margins). Ferris et al. (2000) report that students who received uncoded indirect feedback were nearly as successful (75 percent) at self-correcting errors in revision as those who received coded indirect feedback (77 percent). In a follow-up experimental study, Ferris and Roberts (2001) again found no significant differences in revision success rates between code and no-code treatment groups. Robb, Ross, and Shortreed conclude from their data that for busy writing instructors "less time-consuming methods of directing student attention to surface errors may suffice" (1986, 91). On the other hand, Ferris and Roberts argue that "though the results of this study and the previous two all suggest that a less explicit marking technique may be equally effective in the short-run, this strategy may not give adequate input to produce the reflection and cognitive engagement that helps students to acquire linguistic structures and reduce errors over time" (2001, 177). They suggest that if a clear and consistent system of coded feedback is paired with in-class minilessons that highlight the specific errors being marked, students may show more progress in the long run than if errors are simply underlined. However, at this point in time, there is no evidence to support this speculation.

Effects of Error Feedback across Linguistic Categories

Some researchers have also contrasted the effects of error feedback on student writing across different linguistic categories (lexical, morphological, syntactic). It has been argued that these categories represent completely different domains of linguistic knowledge and that they therefore should not be treated interchangeably by teachers and researchers (Ferris 1999a; Truscott 1996). Indeed, in studies that have isolated specific linguistic constructions for error feedback and analysis, consistent differences have been found in student progress across the various error categories (Chaney 1999; Ferris 1995a; Ferris et al. 2000; Ferris and Roberts 2001; Frantzen 1995; Frantzen and Rissell 1987; Lalande 1982; Sheppard 1992). For instance, in the Ferris et al. (2000) study, students made substantial progress over the course of a semester in reducing

Research Question	Studies Addressing the Question
Does direct or indirect feedback benefit students more?	Ferris et al. 2000; Frantzen 1995; Lalande 1982; Robb, Ross, and Shortreed 1986
Should indirect feedback be coded for error type?	Ferris et al. 2000; Ferris and Roberts 2001; Lalande 1982
Do specific linguistic categories of error respond differently to error feedback?	Chaney 1999; Ferris 1995a; Ferris et al. 2000; Ferris and Roberts 2001; Frantzen 1995; Frantzen and Rissell 1987; Lalande 1982; Sheppard 1992

Fig. 3. Other feedback issues

errors in verb tense and form, made slight progress in reducing lexical and noun ending errors, and regressed (i.e., got worse) in the sentence structure and article errors categories. Figure 3 summarizes studies on types and explicitness of feedback and on the effects of feedback across linguistic categories.

Two relevant distinctions that have been made in the literature are between "global and local" errors and between "treatable and untreatable" errors. The first distinction was introduced by Burt and Kiparsky (1972) to refer to errors that interfere with the comprehensibility of a text (**global errors**) versus more minor errors that do not impede understanding (**local errors**). This dichotomy has been progressively redefined in the subsequent error-correction literature (Bates, Lane, and Lange 1993; Hendrickson 1978), but while it is intuitively appealing, it can be hard to operationalize for research or pedagogical purposes. For instance, Hendrickson (1978) includes some of the same categories as examples of both local and global errors. As noted by Ferris and Hedgcock (1998), it appears that "the *globalness* or seriousness of particular linguistic errors varies from writer to writer and possibly even within a single student text" (205). Further, there is no research evidence to suggest that treating global and local errors differently makes any impact on student writing.

In my response to Truscott 1996 (Ferris 1999a), I introduced the dichotomy between "treatable" and "untreatable" errors as a pedagogical distinction. A **treatable error** is related to a linguistic structure that occurs in a rule-governed way. It is treatable because the student writer can be pointed to a grammar book or set of rules to resolve the problem. An **untreatable error,** on the other hand, is idiosyncratic, and the student will need to utilize acquired knowledge of the language to self-correct it. Examples of treatable errors include verb tense and form; subject-verb agreement; article usage; plural and possessive noun endings; sentence fragments; run-ons and comma splices; some errors in word form; and some errors in punctuation, capitalization, and spelling.[7] Untreatable errors include most word choice errors, with the possible exception of some pronoun and preposition usage, and unidiomatic sentence structure (e.g., problems with word order or with missing or unnecessary words).

Two recent studies have operationalized and examined the "treatable/untreatable" dichotomy. In the first (Ferris et al. 2000), researchers found that teachers were far more likely to give indirect feedback in the case of treatable error types and direct feedback when the error fell into one of the untreatable categories, even though they had agreed at the outset of the study to give coded indirect feedback to all errors that they marked. Remarking on this finding, Chaney (1999) speculates that teachers were operating on an intuitive sense that certain errors were more amenable to self-correction than others. Because of the idiosyncratic nature of untreatable errors, it has been suggested that they are perhaps better addressed with direct feedback (Chaney 1999; Ferris 1999a; Hendrickson 1980).

However, in the second study (Ferris and Roberts 2001), which was a controlled experimental study in which all students received either indirect feedback or none at all, researchers found a more complex picture. While students were more successful at self-editing errors in three treatable categories (verbs, noun endings, and articles) than in the two untreatable categories (word choice and sentence structure), further statistical analysis showed that the differences lay in the sentence structure category, not in the word choice category. In fact, the differences in revision success rates between treatable errors and word choice errors were nonsignificant, and the no-feedback control group was able to self-correct word choice errors better than those in any other category, including all three treatable error categories. And while all students were less successful in correcting sentence structure errors— significantly so—they were still able, as a group, to correct them in 47 percent of the cases, compared with a range of 53 to 60 percent for the other four categories. This suggests that indirect feedback may be useful at least some of the time even in so-called untreatable error categories.[8]

2. What are the effects of other types of classroom intervention on the accuracy of student writing?

Giving students written feedback on their errors is not, of course, the only mechanism writing teachers have available for helping them to improve their accuracy and overall writing quality. Other techniques include teacher-student conferences and peer-editing sessions, revision or rewriting after receiving feedback, in-class grammar instruction tailored to particular problematic issues in writing, and maintenance of error charts or logs so that teachers and students can track progress over time. These various options are further discussed and exemplified in chapter 5. Here we will focus on evaluating the research evidence available on the efficacy of these techniques.

Alternate Forms of Error Feedback

Many writing instructors feel that one-on-one conferences with students, whether to discuss ideas, organization, or errors, are more effective than handwritten commentary or corrections (Zamel 1985). Conferences, after all, offer immediacy and the opportunity for two-way clarification and negotiation. However, there is very little research available about writing conferences with L2 students, and the published studies that do exist (Goldstein and Conrad 1990; Patthey-Chavez and Ferris 1997) do not specifically examine the effects of such conferences on student errors and accuracy. Similarly, both L1 and L2 composition researchers tout the value of peer-response sessions in the writing classroom (see Ferris and Hedgcock 1998 for a review). Although there have been many empirical studies over the past ten years on the nature and effects of peer feedback, none have specifically looked at the effects of peer editing on student accuracy.[9] Thus, though it is certainly possible that both feedback delivery systems (conferences and peer editing), together with rapidly developing technological options such as computer text analyzers or grammar checkers and on-line feedback from instructors and/or peers, may have value in helping students to edit their work and improve the accuracy and clarity of their writing, there is no empirical evidence available to support these assumptions.

Error Correction and Revision

Many researchers have pointed out that teacher feedback of any type is more likely to benefit student writing if it comes primarily at intermediate, rather than final, stages of the writing process—specifically, when students are allowed or even required to revise or rewrite their papers after receiving teacher feedback (Ferris 1995b, 1997; Krashen 1984; James 1998; Zamel 1985). A number of studies already mentioned in this chapter also provide evidence that when students revise their papers after receiving error feedback, their accuracy improves, either in the short or long term (Chandler 2000; Fathman and Whalley 1990; Ferris 1995a, 1997; Ferris et al. 2000; Ferris and Roberts 2001; Frantzen and Rissell 1987; Lalande 1982). On the other hand, in two studies in which one group of students revised their papers while another group did not, there was no benefit as to superior accuracy for the group that revised (Frantzen 1995; Polio, Fleck, and Leder 1998). Finally, in three additional studies the effects of revision are not clear from the data presented (Cohen and Robbins 1976; Semke 1984; Sheppard 1992). It is important to note that in this body of work, only one study specifically isolates revision as a key variable (Chandler 2000). In the rest, other variables in addition to revision differ across groups. For instance, in Lalande's (1982) study, his experimental group received indirect, coded feedback and revised their marked papers during in-class editing sessions, while the control-group students received direct correction and did not revise their papers. Other studies vary along similar lines. In sum, while it seems likely that asking students to edit their papers after receiving error feedback not only will improve the quality of the texts under immediate consideration but will also cause writers to become more aware of and attentive to patterns of error, there is no compelling evidence that the presence or absence of revision makes a difference in the long run. On the other hand, some researchers and reviewers have suggested that revision (along with other forms of writing practice) is the key to long-term student improvement. This is certainly a major area for further research.

In-Class Grammar Instruction

It has also been suggested that writing teachers may need to provide in-class instruction, in the form of grammar mini-lessons and editing-strategy training, to help students learn how to recognize, correct, and avoid various recurring patterns of error (Bates, Lane, and Lange 1993; Byrd and Reid 1998; Ferris 1995c; Ferris and Hedgcock 1998; Frodesen 1991). To my knowledge, there have been no studies that have looked solely at grammar instruction (separate from other variables such as feedback and revision) as a means to improve student accuracy. In several studies in which grammar instruction was intentionally combined with error feedback, students showed progress in written accuracy (Ferris 1995a; Frantzen and Rissell 1987; Lalande 1982), but in other studies it did not appear to make a difference or to help students (Frantzen 1995; Polio, Fleck, and Leder 1998). Most experts on the teaching of grammar to L2 students agree that classroom grammar instruction is most effective when it is carefully paired with opportunities for students to apply what they have learned to their own output. In the context of grammar and editing minilessons in the writing class, the most obvious applications would be for students to practice newly covered grammatical concepts by finding and correcting errors in sample student texts and then in their own texts (see chap. 5 for further details). While it seems clear that grammar instruction alone is unlikely to help most student writers improve, what is unknown from the research base is whether carefully planned minilessons that are keyed to real student writing problems and explicitly connected to other forms of intervention (such as feedback and revision exercises) will provide additional support that is needed for at least some students to improve their writing. Again, the research evidence is inconclusive because grammar instruction has not been isolated from other pedagogical techniques and because the nature of the grammar instruction itself is almost never specified in the research reports.

Error Logs

It has also been suggested that long-term progress in accuracy can be facilitated by the maintenance of error logs or charts by teachers and/or students themselves (Bates, Lane, and Lange 1993; Ferris 1995a, 1995c; Lalande 1982). Error logs help students to focus on major patterns of written error and to be aware of the relative frequency of various error types as they move from one draft or assignment to the next in a writing class. Two studies to date have investigated the usefulness of error logs for L2 student writers (Ferris and Helt 2000; Komura 1999; Lalande 1982; Roberts 1999).[10] In Lalande's (1982) study, the experimental group received indirect coded feedback, did in-class revisions immediately after their marked papers were returned, and maintained error logs, outperforming the control group, which received direct correction and in-class grammar instruction. Lalande reports that the experimental group significantly outperformed the control group on accuracy measures at the end of the semester. However, because the two groups varied in at least four different ways (type of error feedback received, revision, in-class grammar instruction, and maintenance of error logs), it is difficult to isolate the effects of error logs. In contrast, studies completed by Komura (1999), Roberts (1999), and Ferris and Helt (2000) analyzed data from groups of student writers that varied only along the error-log variable. While Komura's and Roberts's studies showed no short-term benefits for error logs (i.e., no revision success from one draft to the next of the same paper), Ferris and Helt's longitudinal analysis showed a clear advantage for the error-log group from the beginning to the end of the semester. As noted by Roberts (1999), there were a number of technical problems with the design and implementation of the error logs. These included the use of too many error categories and codes, representing in some cases grammar terminology and rules with which the student writers were not familiar; lack of integration of the error logs into other classroom activities; and lack of consistency on the part of teachers and students in maintaining the logs. It is possible that if these problems had been resolved, maintenance of error logs might have shown greater benefit for the students. However, the research database is far too small to draw any conclusions about the possible usefulness of error logs. Figure 4 outlines the previous research on the effects of various types of error treatment on student writing.

3. What are students' views and perceptions about error treatment in their writing?

In addition to examining empirical research evidence about the nature and effects of error feedback and other types of instructional intervention, it is important to consider student preferences and expectations. It has been assumed in the literature that L2 student writers expect and value error feedback from their teachers, and it has been claimed that the absence of such feedback could raise student anxiety, frustrate students, and cause them to lose confidence in their teachers

Research Question	Studies Addressing the Question
Does revision after feedback help students make progress in accuracy?	Chandler 2000; Cohen and Robbins 1976; Fathman and Whalley 1990; Ferris 1995a, 1997; Ferris et al. 2000; Ferris and Roberts 2001; Frantzen 1995; Frantzen and Rissell 1987; Lalande 1982; Polio, Fleck, and Leder 1998; Semke 1984; Sheppard 1992
Does in-class grammar instruction benefit student writers?	Ferris 1995a; Frantzen 1995; Frantzen and Rissell 1987; Lalande 1982; Polio, Fleck, and Leder 1998
Does maintenance of error logs help students to improve their writing?	Ferris and Helt 2000; Komura 1999; Lalande 1982; Roberts 1999

Fig. 4. Studies of other types of error treatment

(Ferris 1999a; Ferris and Hedgcock 1998; Frantzen 1995; Leki 1991). On the other hand, some have claimed that excessive attention to student errors may be offensive and demotivating to student writers and that it may be ultimately harmful to them because it deflects teacher and student time and attention away from more important aspects of writing, such as process, development of ideas, and organization (Krashen 1984; Truscott 1996; Zamel 1985).

A number of surveys of student opinion over the past decade or so have looked at issues surrounding feedback in general and error correction in particular. These are summarized in figure 5. These studies have ranged from case studies (Brice 1995; Cohen and Cavalcanti 1990; Roberts 1999) to large-scale surveys with more than 300 subjects (e.g., Hedgcock and Lefkowitz 1994; Rennie 2000). In several cases, larger-scale questionnaire studies were combined with interviews of a smaller sample of subjects (e.g., Hedgcock and Lefkowitz 1996; Komura 1999). This body of work can be subdivided into two larger categories (see fig. 5): (1) studies that assess student

Study Focus	Specific References
Student views on writing issues to be covered in teacher feedback (e.g., ideas, organization, grammar)	Cohen 1987; Cohen and Cavalcanti 1990; Enginarlar 1993; Ferris 1995b; Hedgcock and Lefkowitz 1994, 1996; Radecki and Swales 1988
Student views on specific grammar-feedback mechanisms and options	Brice 1995; Ferris et al. 2000; Ferris and Roberts 2001; Hedgcock and Lefkowitz 1994, 1996; Komura 1999; Leki 1991; Radecki and Swales 1988; Rennie 2000; Roberts 1999

Fig. 5. Summary of student survey research on feedback and error correction

opinions and preferences about teacher feedback in general, touching upon error correction and grammar issues in conjunction with other questions; and (2) research that looks primarily at error correction in student writing, examining not only student opinions about the relative value of such feedback but specific student views about how error correction should be delivered by teachers.

In the first group of studies, student survey respondents, typically university ESL students in the United States (but also foreign language subjects in the studies by Cohen [1997] and Hedgcock and Lefkowitz [1994, 1996]), were asked about the relative merits of various types of feedback. Specifically, they were asked whether they received and/or preferred to receive feedback about content, organization, grammar, vocabulary, and mechanics. Somewhat to the dismay of the researchers in some cases, a strong and consistent preference for grammar feedback on the part of L2 student writers was found. Both Radecki and Swales (1988) and Leki (1991) note the conflict between students' strong desire for grammar feedback and existing research evidence that suggested that error correction was not only ineffectual but perhaps even harmful to the development of student writing. While both sets of authors suggest that writing teachers share with students the research about the limitations of error correction and the benefits of the process approach, Leki also points out that "it seems at best counter-productive, at worst high-handed and disrespectful of our students, to simply insist that they trust our preferences. . . . [W]e do well at least to become aware of students' perceptions of their needs and their sense of what helps them progress" (1991, 210). Lending support to Leki's observations is a recent study by Brice and Newman (2000), in which a writing teacher provided students with no error feedback at all. Though the teacher did a good job of explaining her rationale for this to the students and though the students liked and respected the teacher, they did express a consistent and mounting sense of frustration and anxiety about the lack of form-focused feedback. The authors conclude that it may be very difficult to ignore or change L2 students' views about the importance of error feedback from their writing teachers.

Later researchers, however, note that student writers in process-oriented composition classes claimed to value feedback of all types, not just on their errors (Ferris 1995b; Hedgcock and Lefkowitz 1994, 1996). Another consistent finding across this group of studies is that instructors' priorities, as expressed through their feedback, appeared to influence students' perceptions and attitudes about the types of issues they wanted addressed through teacher feedback. In other words, if a teacher primarily gave feedback about surface-level error, that teacher's students were likely to say that they preferred to receive feedback about their errors. In general, there appeared to be a good match between what students said they wanted in teacher feedback and the types of feedback they reported receiving from their teachers.

Finally, in this body of studies, there appears to be little support for assertions from L1 researchers that student writers ignore and resent teacher feedback, especially if it focuses on form and errors. As pointed out by Leki (1990, 1991), L2 writers have linguistic and rhetorical deficits when compared to L1 writers. Further, they may have an "overriding sense of urgency to perfect their English" paired with "less reluctance to have errors pointed out" because they do not have the same sense of stigma connected with their problems in formal written English that L1 student writers may feel (Leki 1991, 205).

In the second group of studies, students were asked specifically about the types of error feedback they found most helpful. Though different questions were asked in the various studies, some generalizations may be made. First, to the extent students complained about or had problems with teacher error correction, such problems were often connected to "implicit" suggestions (Brice 1995; Radecki and Swales 1988) such as underlining, arrows, boxes, circles, and error codes such as "vt" (verb tense) or "ro" (run-on). While students in general claimed to have little trouble understanding and utilizing teacher feedback, when they were confused, such teacher notations and shorthand were most typically the culprits. Second, students appeared to be open to a cooperative approach to error feedback in which the teacher called attention to errors through locating and labeling them but then left it to the student to attempt to make the correction in a rewrite or revision. It seemed clear from a number of disparate studies that students recognized that they were likely to learn more and become more independent as writers and editors if they had some investment in the process, rather than simply copying or noting direct corrections the teachers had made.

Third, students were uniformly hostile to error-correction approaches in which the teacher did not mark errors at all but left it to the writers to find, diagnose, and solve problems by themselves. For instance, in studies by Leki (1991), Ferris and Roberts (2001), and Rennie (2000), when students were asked if they preferred teachers not to mark errors at all, no students chose this option in the first two studies and only two students (.6 percent) of Rennie's subjects said they would like this scenario (see also Brice and Newman 2000). However, there was more variety in student responses as to whether error correction should be comprehensive (covering all errors found) or selective (focusing on the most frequent and serious errors). While the majority of students in these studies claimed to favor comprehensive correction, there was a noticeable minority that appeared to see merit in selective correction, as long as it dealt with the "most serious" errors.

Two other issues were addressed in a couple of the survey studies. As previously mentioned, when students were asked whether they preferred errors to be labeled or just located, they strongly favored errors to be labeled by type (Ferris et al. 2000; Ferris and Roberts 2001; Hedgcock and Lefkowitz 1994, 1996; Rennie 2000). However, as already discussed, there is to this point no evidence that this more precise labeling of errors makes a difference in students' short- or long-term progress in accuracy (Ferris et al. 2000; Ferris and Roberts 2001; Robb, Ross, and Shortreed 1986). The other question concerned the teacher's use of a red pen to mark errors, a technique that has been discouraged by L1 and L2 composition experts as being too negative and intimidating to students (seen as the teacher "bleeding all over" the student's paper). Two studies (Hedgcock and Lefkowitz 1994, 1996; Leki 1991) investigated this question in student surveys. In neither case did they find that their L2 subjects had strongly negative feelings about the color of ink the teacher used to mark errors.

What is notable about this body of student-opinion studies is how consistent the findings are, despite variations in methodology and in subject characteristics. To summarize these two related lines of research, studies of student opinion about teacher feedback have consistently found the following:

- students feel that teacher feedback on grammar and errors is extremely important to their progress as writers;
- students in the most recent studies also see value in other types of teacher feedback (on ideas and organization);
- student writers mostly favor comprehensive teacher marking of errors;
- student writers, when given a choice of teacher marking strategies, tend to prefer that teachers mark errors and give them strategies for correcting them over either direct correction of errors or less explicit indirect methods;

- students sometimes found teachers' marking systems confusing or cumbersome.

4. What research questions need to be further explored?

A review of research and issues such as the one in this chapter often seems to raise more questions than it answers. By looking critically at an existing body of studies, we become aware (often painfully so) of the gaps in the empirical evidence on a particular topic and of the inadequacies of some of the previous lines of research. Some possible research questions that arise from the foregoing review are outlined in figure 6 and then discussed briefly.

One vitally important issue to examine is research methodology. For instance, the various studies on the effects of error-correction methods have typically looked at extremely diverse student populations, ranging from American college students taking foreign language classes (sometimes as majors, sometimes not) at U.S. universities to immigrant ESL writers who have learned English primarily through acquisition and exposure to the language rather than through formal training. Not only do subject characteristics differ on about every parameter imaginable, but their motivation and purposes for studying the language and developing their L2 writing skills are likely to be very different as well (Ferris 1999b; Hedgcock and Lefkowitz 1994; Reid 1998a). Yet in many reviews of research, studies that include subjects of widely varying characteristics are treated as though they are looking at the same populations. Similar concerns can be raised about other design issues, including the characteristics of the error feedback and who was providing it; the types of student writing being considered; the types of linguistic issues covered; and methodological points such as inclusion of control groups, baseline pretreatment data, and reporting of interrater reliabilities. While it is hardly controversial to point out that such issues need to be considered both in designing primary research and in evaluating and

1. Do students who receive consistent and accurate error feedback over time improve in written accuracy more than comparable students who receive no error feedback?

2. Does indirect feedback help students more than direct feedback?

3. Does indirect feedback need to be coded or labeled by error type to be most helpful to students, or is error labeling adequate?

4. Should error feedback be comprehensive or selective?

5. Should all error types be given indirect feedback, or are there particular linguistic issues best treated by direct feedback?

6. Are students at lower levels of L2 proficiency better served by direct feedback than by indirect feedback?

7. Does required revision or rewriting after feedback help students to improve in accuracy more than feedback alone?

8. Does in-class grammar instruction help students to improve in written accuracy?

9. Does maintenance of error logs help students to improve in accuracy?

10. Are students better served by having error feedback tailored to their stated individual preferences?

11. What individual student variables affect student uptake of error feedback, and how can the writing instructor utilize or mitigate the effects of these variables?

Fig. 6. Possible research questions for future inquiry

reviewing secondary research, it is important to mention here because many studies fail to control for or even consider these questions. Future research studies, and undoubtedly further reviews of research, need to examine design and methodology issues with far more care than has been demonstrated to this point.

The review in this chapter has itself raised a number of questions regarding error correction in L2 student writing that need more attention than they have received to date. Most crucially, there need to be longitudinal, contextualized studies that examine the effects of error correction on students' language control, written accuracy, and writing quality. The writing of students who receive consistent, thoughtful, and accurate error feedback needs to be compared with the writing of students who receive other forms of writing instruction but no error correction. It should be frankly noted that it can be very difficult to conduct such studies, since both teachers and students have such strong biases as to the necessity for error correction that teachers would feel remiss if they did not provide it—and, perhaps more to the point, would fear hostility from their students (Truscott 1996, 1999). Nonetheless, a compelling case for or against error correction in L2 writing classes cannot possibly be made without a substantial body of research studies along these lines.

Inextricable from the critical question—does error correction help students to improve their writing?—is the question of what makes error feedback effective or ineffective. As I have noted elsewhere (Ferris 1999a; Ferris and Hedgcock 1998), few would argue that poorly conceived, inconsistent, or inaccurate error correction is likely to help student writers; it may well be harmful to their development. Though the answers to this question bear much more scrutiny, we at least have some starting points from the available research: (1) indirect feedback is in most cases preferable to direct feedback; (2) a wide range of error types, including those previously deemed "untreatable," appear to be responsive to indirect feedback; and (3) coded, labeled feedback may not be necessary in some cases. While more research should be conducted to examine all three of the above generalizations with a range of student populations and in a variety of contexts, it may be most helpful from this point to examine feedback in conjunction with other types of error treatment discussed in this review—revision, grammar instruction, and the use of error logs. It would also be informative to look at whether students who are at relatively low levels of L2 proficiency benefit from different types of feedback (e.g., direct correction followed by rewriting) and error treatment than those who are more advanced (Ferris and Hedgcock 1998).

A final direction for further research on error treatment arises from the body of work on student views of teacher feedback.

It has been suggested that student writers be offered a range of feedback options by their teachers and that feedback be individually tailored to their preferences. Appealing as this suggestion may be from a humanistic, affective perspective, it certainly sounds challenging and cumbersome for teachers, and there is no empirical evidence to suggest that such accommodations make a difference, compared with teachers simply providing feedback in way(s) they deem best. However, other lines of research on error correction and second language acquisition do indicate that there is a great deal of individual variation in students' ability to process teacher feedback and utilize it for their development as writers. Such variation may come from the nature of the students' L1s; their prior exposure to the L2 and to composition instruction; and their motivation, personality, and learning style. The sources and implications of individual student variation in response to error treatment have not begun to receive serious investigation or attention. Perhaps these two lines of inquiry—focusing on stated student preferences and individual differences—can help teachers to understand better why some students make substantial progress while others make less (or none at all) in response to feedback and to tailor error-treatment strategies accordingly.

Chapter 3

Preparing L2 Writing Teachers to Treat Student Error

For many ESL writing instructors, the prospect of responding to students' errors (chap. 4) or providing strategy training and grammar instruction (chap. 5) may appear rather daunting. Not only does the teacher need to sort through a range of pedagogical options, materials, and techniques, but effective treatment of error also requires that instructors have solid linguistic knowledge and analysis skills themselves. The purpose of this chapter is to discuss *what* L2 writing teachers need to know about grammar, and *how* they can acquire such knowledge and build their skills.

It is important to acknowledge that unless L2 teachers specifically make the effort to prepare themselves to deal with student errors, they may do so less effectively than they should. In Truscott's (1996) critique of grammar correction in the L2 writing class, he discusses teachers' lack of knowledge and preparation under the rubric of "practical problems" that impede even the potential effectiveness of error feedback.

> First, the teacher must realize that a mistake has been made. The well-known problems involved in proof-reading show that this step cannot be taken for granted. . . . If teachers do recognize an error, they still may not have a good understanding of the correct use—questions regarding grammar can be very difficult, even for experts, and someone who writes or speaks English well does not necessarily understand the principles involved. . . . Thus, teachers may well know that an error has occurred but not know exactly why

it is an error. If they do understand it well, they might be unable to give a good explanation; problems that need explaining are often very complex. (350–51)

Though it is quite easy to recognize the truth in Truscott's dismal assessment, it is important to observe that the situation is not quite as hopeless as it may seem. Also, as discussed in chapter 2, there is actually limited empirical evidence to back up Truscott's claims that teacher feedback is inaccurate and incomplete.

In the MA TESOL graduate program in which I teach, my colleagues and I became concerned a few years ago with our students' inability to provide adequate analyses of language errors in sample student papers. Their inadequacies were revealed through course projects in our classes in pedagogical grammar and in the teaching of writing, in their on-campus work as tutors and teaching assistants, and in comprehensive examination questions in which they were given student papers and asked to analyze written errors. Since our graduate program emphasizes the teaching of English in primarily academic settings, we felt that the performance of our students demonstrated serious shortcomings in the ways that we prepared them to deal with this crucial issue. In response, we developed a comprehensive training program to help our MA students better cope with grammar issues in general and student writing in particular.[1] Results of a pilot study (Ferris, Harvey, and Nuttall 1998) suggest that 12 graduate students who participated in a semester-long grammar training and tutoring project substantially improved in their ability to identify errors in sample student writing. The trainees' journal entries also reflected a growing confidence in their ability to teach grammar to ESL writers and to explain difficult concepts to them as they gained experience in doing so both from prepared lesson materials and from on-the-spot questions and explanations.

Our TESOL program's revamped training sequence now includes the following components:

1. Prerequisite undergraduate courses in linguistics and grammar (most notably a newly developed course entitled "Grammar for ESL Teaching," which is distinct from our department's English-major course called "Traditional Grammar and Standard Usage")

2. Required graduate courses in pedagogical grammar and in the teaching of writing, both of which include assignments in which MA students must analyze ESL student error, develop lesson plans to address errors, and become familiar with student grammar textbooks and other materials

3. A newly developed component of the required practicum course in which students must teach six-week (12 contact hours) small-group tutorials on grammar for ESL writers. Lesson plans and materials are provided for them so that they can learn from working through the materials and responding to the lessons.

Since we implemented these changes in 1997, we have noticed steady improvement in our graduate students' ability to assess language problems in both ESL student writing and in speaking. While these observations are anecdotal, they do suggest that providing future teachers with adequate preparation and practice for addressing grammar issues can yield immediate benefits (which we presume also help them when they are in their own classrooms after graduating from our program).

Obviously, not all TESOL preparation programs may have the opportunity or resources to implement the changes that we have been able to. Nor do revamped preservice training protocols benefit in-service teachers already in the field. Nonetheless, the revision process that our MA program has undergone can help to isolate some principles that are applicable to both preservice and in-service L2 writing instructors elsewhere. Following is further discussion of these principles.

Principle 1. Teachers of ESL writing need to study aspects of grammar that are particularly problematic for nonnative speakers of English.

Studies of errors made by student writers who are native speakers of English have highlighted issues such as punctuation of sentences and clauses, pronoun reference, modification problems, and lexical errors indicating that students are selecting more casual registers than are allowed in formal written English (see Weaver 1996 for a review). While L2 writers may also have trouble with commas, apostrophes, semicolons, pronouns, and informal usage, their more serious issues are related to language structures that are almost never problematic for native speakers. These include verb tense and aspect issues, the use of articles and other determiners, noun endings (plural and possessive inflectional endings), errors in word form (such as using a noun form where an adjective is required), and word order. To be able to recognize such errors in written discourse and to address them in talking to students, prospective ESL teachers need to acquire substantial knowledge of the following issues:

- the forms, meanings, and uses of the different verb tense and aspect combinations in English;
- the forms, meanings, and uses of active and passive voice constructions;
- the basic verb types (transitive, intransitive, and linking) and the constraints on each type as to passivization, addition of direct objects, etc.;
- the auxiliary forms that can be added to verb phrases and the effects of auxiliaries on the use of inflectional morphemes (i.e., tense/aspect markers) in the verb phrase;
- the basic types of nouns (abstract, concrete, collective, count, noncount) and the implications of these types for article usage and inflectional endings;
- the general rules governing subject-verb agreement;

- the differences in meaning and use between definite and indefinite articles;
- basic clause and sentence patterns and how they should be combined and punctuated;
- differences in form and function between nouns, verbs, adjectives, and adverbs and how to select the correct form when constructing a sentence.

While this list will certainly not cover all of the possible problems that ESL learners may encounter with English grammar, it addresses the most frequent and serious issues found in ESL student writing (see chap. 4, especially table 1, for further discussion of common ESL errors).

Current or prospective teachers who are unable to take a course that specifically prepares them to deal with these linguistic issues may wish to acquire a reference library that explains these various constructions either for teachers or for students themselves. It is helpful to have available both one or more teacher-reference grammars and several ESL grammar textbooks, the former for the depth of explanation and illustrations that teachers need to be well prepared and the latter to give instructors a sense of how much information to present to students.

The Potential Benefits of Corpus Linguistics

A recent area of much research is corpus linguistics with pedagogical applications. In corpus linguistics, large quantities of texts in the target language are computer-analyzed for relative frequencies of specific lexical items and morphological and syntactic constructions (e.g., Biber 1988; Biber et al. 1999). The potential application of this line of research to the L2 classroom is that it highlights the vocabulary and grammar to which students will be exposed and/or that they may need to learn to produce. It has been suggested, for example, that writing teachers analyze the vocabulary and syntax of college textbooks in various disciplines so that they can create genre-specific materials for students in their classes (Byrd 1998; Schleppe-grell 1998). Corpus linguistics, while an interesting area of research, requires a relatively high level of technical expertise on the part of the researcher or teacher who would like to utilize it. Still, resources such as Biber et al.'s (1999) corpus-based discourse grammar may prove to be immensely useful to writing teachers as descriptive and classroom research progresses.

> **Principle 2. Teachers need practice in recognizing and identifying errors in student writing.**

A novice teacher of L2 writing may become easily overwhelmed by the language problems in students' texts, especially if the students are at fairly low levels of second language proficiency. It is worth the time and effort to work with a more experienced writing teacher or teacher educator to practice identifying, classifying, and correcting errors in a set of student papers. This can happen either formally, in a class on teaching grammar or writing or in a practicum setting, or informally, as a teacher who needs experience in this area apprentices herself or himself to a more experienced writing instructor. For my own graduate course entitled "Teaching ESL Writing," I have developed several in-class and out-of-class exercises to help my preservice MA students build their error-analysis skills. These exercises are shown in figure 7.

> **Principle 3. Teachers need practice in developing lessons and teaching grammar points to their ESL writing students.**

As discussed in chapter 5, in-class grammar minilessons can help students to understand the rules and issues surrounding points of English grammar that are troublesome for L2 student writers (e.g., when to use simple past vs. present perfect tenses;

IN-CLASS WORKSHOP: ANALYZING STUDENT ERRORS AND GIVING FEEDBACK

Instructions

(a) Read the essay on the attached pages (two copies provided). Complete the error-analysis form that follows.

(b) Use your completed analysis to give feedback in two different ways:

  (1) **on copy 1,** mark the errors you identified using the error codes in figure 12 on page 69;

  (2) **on copy 2,** construct an end note to the student on which you tell him or her about the two or three most prevalent error patterns in the paper (based upon your analysis). Then go through and underline each example of the errors you've selected.

Do this exercise individually; you'll discuss the follow-up questions in small groups.

Follow-Up Questions

(1) What were the major patterns of error you found during your analysis?

(2) What difficulties (if any) did you experience in either analyzing the errors or marking the essay excerpt?

(3) Which of the two feedback procedures did you find easier to do? Which one did you like better? Which do you think would help students more? Why?

OUT-OF-CLASS ASSIGNMENT: ANALYSIS OF STUDENT ESSAYS

Attached are two student papers, both written for an advanced university ESL course. Read each one carefully, paying attention to the various error types represented in each paper. Then complete the tasks described below.

1. Develop an error-analysis form reflecting the major types of error you notice in the two papers. You may wish to add or delete error categories, depending upon your preliminary reading of the papers.

2. Make two copies of the form and complete an error analysis for each paper.

3. Now imagine that you are going to give each of the two student writers feedback about his or her grammar problems. Considering the principles for grammar feedback we have discussed, mark the papers as though you were going to return them to the students for final editing.

Submit:
  • your two error-analysis forms (steps 1–2);
  • your two marked essays (you will need to make copies of these for your journal) (step 3);
  • a one- to two-page reflection on your error-analysis/correction processes.

Fig. 7. Sample error-analysis exercises for a teacher-preparation course. (The assignment is adapted from Application Activity 7.3 in Ferris and Hedgcock 1998, 352–53.)

when to use definite, indefinite, or zero articles in noun phrases). As mentioned above, in our MA TESOL program, we have developed a six-week, 12-hour grammar tutorial program that is a component of our required practicum. In this grammar tutorial (taught by the practicum students for two hours per week to groups of 6 to 12 ESL writers), tutors are given a complete set of lesson plans and other materials to use. These materials serve as models for the preservice teachers of how to select and narrow key grammar points, define terms and explain and exemplify rules, and use text-analysis and editing practice exercises to help students apply the concepts they have learned (see chap. 5, especially figs. 18 and 19 and apps. 5D and 5E, for more examples and discussion). Further, because student questions that are not covered in the lesson plans inevitably arise, tutors gain additional in-the-trenches experience in explaining points of grammar. During this six-week tutorial program, the practicum supervisor meets regularly with the tutors to go over lesson plans and discuss any questions or problems; the supervisor also observes each student at least once in the classroom. Tutors are also encouraged to use the class list-serve to bring up any grammar questions or problems with lesson plans that arise in their tutorials for input from other tutors, from the practicum instructor, and from other faculty in the MA TESOL program.

In addition to this highly structured, closely supervised practicum experience, MA TESOL students are required to complete a number of projects that require them to apply the knowledge and experience they are acquiring to develop their own materials. These projects occur in conjunction with the practicum course and the required MA courses in teaching ESL writing and in pedagogical grammar and occasionally as part of the MA TESOL comprehensive examination. Students must, for instance, complete a detailed error analysis of a set of student papers, look through several grammar textbooks to develop a minilesson on a selected grammar point, and examine a set of 10 student papers to find appropriate models for text-analysis exercises to be used in conjunction with a grammar minilesson. The appendix to chapter 3 provides examples of these assignments.

> **Principle 4. Teachers need to understand the principles of second language acquisition and of composition theory.**

This chapter thus far has focused on building teachers' knowledge of specific grammatical concepts and of techniques for responding to student error and teaching grammar to student writers. However, it is also important that such teacher awareness be embedded in the big picture of second language acquisition theory—in the knowledge that mastery of second language forms and structures takes considerable time and may well not happen for many adult learners without effective instruction, that differences between L1 and L2 forms may lead to student errors in writing, and that individual differences in learning styles and motivation may affect students' responsiveness to grammar-teaching techniques and to editing-strategy training. Preservice teachers should ideally have both introductory and advanced coursework in second language acquisition theory that covers acquisition processes and individual differences, among other issues. Practicing teachers should be familiar with books and articles that emphasize or include the applications of SLA theory to the teaching and learning of grammar (e.g., Ellis 1998; Doughty and Williams 1998).

Beyond considering the implications of SLA theory and research for the teaching of grammar, ESL writing teachers need to keep grammar and error issues firmly in perspective. As L1 and L2 composition and writing theorists have reminded us, there are many issues beyond error that should concern L2 writers and their teachers. After all, the frequency of errors in a student text is not the sole or even the most important indicator of overall writing quality. Process-approach advocates remind us that students learn simply from the process and practice of writing and that we should facilitate and mediate these processes and help the students not to short-circuit their thinking because of premature and excessive attention to forms and errors (Krashen 1984; Sommers 1982; Spack 1988; Zamel 1982, 1985). Scholars in contrastive rhetoric point out that, to the degree their texts sound "wrong," L2 students may be utilizing thinking and rhetorical patterns from their L1 traditions rather than simply making mistakes in the L2 (Connor 1996; Connor and Kaplan 1987; Kaplan 1966). Experts in genre analysis suggest that rather than analyzing linguistic forms and errors in isolation, we consider the purposes for which student texts are being produced and examine the forms and structures students need to understand and master in order to communicate most effectively for their target audience (e.g., Connor and Johns 1990; Johns 1997; Swales 1990). Writing teachers, therefore, as they consider the treatment of error in student writing, need to consider its relative importance in student writing processes and products and the impact of L1 knowledge and literacy experience on error. While we should not neglect attention to student accuracy and clarity in writing, we also should not give it *more* attention than it deserves. Accuracy concerns should at all times be carefully balanced with development of students' ideas and rhetorical strategies as well as consideration of the (in)effectiveness of their own writing processes.

Summary

Over the years I have worked in a TESOL teacher preparation program, my colleagues and I, on a regular basis, have fielded office visits, phone calls, and E-mail inquiries that begin as follows: "In 25 words or fewer, can you tell me how to teach English as a Second Language?" or "I've just been hired to teach English abroad in (*fill in name of country*), and I have neither the time for nor interest in obtaining any training before I go. What materials or resources can you recommend for me?" My typical response to such questions is something like "You wouldn't expect to go practice medicine or program computers without any training, even though you've been to the doctor and used a computer, would you? There is more to teaching English (or any other language) effectively than just knowing how to speak English. If you want to do it well, you will have to undertake a program of preparation."

This advice (which nearly all of these walk-ins ignore, by the way) holds true especially for writing teachers who want to treat student error effectively. Being a fairly competent user of the English language does not in and of itself prepare teachers to diagnose and respond to student error and to explain grammatical concepts in English. I can attest to this firsthand, as can any experienced ESL writing teacher. As an undergraduate English major, I won academic honors from my university and my department. I was an extremely proficient writer who rarely made a mistake in grammar or spelling (even before computers). But during my first year in an MA TESOL graduate program, I was tutoring ESL writers in our campus writing center. I vividly remember being asked something innocuous like "What's the difference between a direct and indirect object?" and realizing that *I had no idea what the answer was!* I could use the language accurately myself, and I could find errors in student writing and suggest correct forms. But I could not explain to the students why the form was wrong and how to avoid such errors the next time they wrote. My panicked response was to sign up for an English grammar class (which was not even required for MA TESOL students!) the very next semester.

My own experience as a teacher and as a teacher educator convinces me that ESL writing teachers *can and should* learn to treat student errors effectively. In-service teachers who are beyond their own teacher preparation programs may need to do some reading, to audit a grammar class, to attend workshops or conference presentations on grammar teaching, or to apprentice themselves to a more experienced teacher who can mentor them in analyzing and responding to student errors and in classroom grammar instruction. Before we can prepare our students to cope with errors in their writing, we must prepare ourselves.

Chapter 4
Responding to Student Errors: Issues and Strategies

As we have seen, there has been some confusion—and even controversy—about whether teachers ought to mark student errors at all. Process advocates have argued that excessive attention to student errors may short-circuit students' writing and thinking process, making writing only an exercise in practicing grammar and vocabulary rather than a way to discover and express meaning (Zamel 1982, 1985). Some error-correction researchers and reviewers have examined the not-very-encouraging evidence about the effects of grammar feedback on student development and concluded that it is a waste of teacher energy and deflects student attention from more important issues (Krashen 1984; Truscott 1996, 1999).

However, as previously noted, there is both empirical and anecdotal evidence to indicate that *well-constructed* error feedback, especially when combined with judiciously delivered strategy training and grammar minilessons (see chap. 5), is not only highly valued by students but may also be of great benefit to their development as writers and to their overall second language acquisition (Bates, Lane, and Lange 1993; Ellis 1998; Ferris 1995b, 1997, 1999b; Ferris and Hedgcock 1998). This chapter, therefore, proceeds on the assumption that teacher-supplied error feedback may be extremely beneficial to ESL student writers and explores various practical issues raised by the endeavor of providing such feedback.

- *Which errors* should be corrected?
- *When* should error feedback be provided?
- *How* should teachers give error feedback?

- How can teachers help students to *process and utilize* error feedback effectively?
- How can ESL writing teachers *use their time wisely and avoid burnout* in giving error feedback?

Choosing Which Errors to Mark: Comprehensive versus Selective Error Correction

Many advocates of error correction warn against attempting to mark *all* student errors because of the very real risk of exhausting teachers and overwhelming students. In a large-scale study by Ferris et al. (2000), the three ESL composition teachers who were attempting to mark and code nearly all of the student errors in conjunction with the research project would sometimes mark well over 100 errors on one two- to three-page (slightly under 800 words) paper—and yet the researchers noted that the instructors did not, despite their best efforts, catch all of the students' errors! It has also been suggested that error feedback may be most effective when it focuses on **patterns of error**, allowing teachers and students to attend to, say, two or three major error types at a time, rather than dozens of disparate errors. This selective error-correction strategy helps students learn to make focused passes through their texts to find particular types of errors to which they may be most prone and to master grammatical terms and rules related to those specific errors (see chap. 5).

Secondly, teachers need to distinguish in their own minds and in their marking strategies between **errors** and **stylistic differences**. Because ESL writing teachers are usually either native speakers of English or highly proficient nonnative speakers, as readers they are likely to be sensitive not only to morphological, lexical, syntactic, and mechanical errors but also to wording that could be improved or wording or phrasing that is not exactly wrong but is not precisely the way a native speaker might say it, either. Nonetheless, it is probably best for teachers to focus most of their efforts in marking and teaching on errors rather than improvement of writing style, except for very advanced students who make few errors. With a few exceptions (e.g., when to use active or passive voice and informal pronoun usage [e.g., "one" vs. "you"]), writing style more likely comes from exposure to the target language (especially written language) than from correction or classroom instruction. Teachers' energies and student attention are better spent on more explicit issues about which rules can be taught and learned and student progress can be observed. While in some instances the line between an error and a style distinction can be quite blurry (see fig. 8 for examples), teachers need to be thoughtful in such cases about which items to mark and which to leave alone.

That said, in endeavoring to mark papers judiciously and selectively, how do teachers go about selecting which errors to mark? The answer to this question lies in several stages.

Stage 1. Understand the types of errors that are most common to ESL writers.

While native-English-speaking students struggle with issues like punctuation rules, pronoun reference, and informal usage in their academic writing (Weaver 1996), ESL writers make different types of errors. Though error types will obviously vary across L1s, learner proficiency levels, and other student characteristics, the list of error types given in table 1 (taken from Ferris et al. 2000) is fairly representative of what researchers, teachers, and textbook authors have found and emphasized in giving error feedback to ESL writers. Appendix 4A provides brief explanations and illustrations of each error type.

In considering this list, or others like it, it is important to recognize several issues. First, errors made by students represent different types of linguistic knowledge. Table 1 shows that the errors marked in this fairly large corpus were spread across morphological, lexical, syntactic, and mechanical categories. Truscott (1996) has argued that different types of errors may need varying treatment in terms of error correction, an issue often overlooked by teachers and textbook developers.

Errors

1. *Original student text:* In addition **of** the challenge . . .

   Teacher correction: In addition **to** the challenge . . .

2. *Original student text:* **Even** *they are not truly happy in here, but they still . . .*

   wc [word choice]
   Teacher correction: <u>Even</u> *they* . . .

3. *Original student text: There are a lot of problems such **like** family tradition . . .*

   as
   Teacher correction: There are a lot of problems such ~~like~~ family tradition . . .

Style Differences

1. *Original student text: It shows **that** culture, custom and language* **identify our identity.**

   our?
   Teacher correction: It shows ~~that~~ culture, custom and language
   to others
   ~~identify our identity.~~

2. *Original student text:* **Therefore, I** *have hope that it would lead me to success.*

   I, too,
   Teacher correction: ~~Therefore, I~~ *have hope that it would lead me to success.*

3. *Original student text: As I observe some teachers here they do not have much respect for their **parents** and elders. In **addition,** they usually talk back to **their parents.***

   fact,
   Teacher correction: In **~~addition,~~** *they usually talk back to*
   them
   ~~their parents.~~

Fig. 8. Errors versus style distinctions: sample sentences with teacher corrections. *Note:* The examples represent actual teacher corrections and are used for illustrative purposes only. It should not be assumed that these (sometimes overly directive) responses are recommended. (All examples taken from Ferris et al. 2000 research corpus.)

TABLE 1. Common ESL Writing Errors

Error Type	*Percentage of Total Errors Marked*
Morphological Errors	
Verbs	
Tense	10.9
Form	7.8
Subject-verb agreement	2.9
Total Verb Errors	**21.6**
Nouns	
Articles/determiners	6.6
Noun endings (plural/possessive)	8.9
Total Noun Errors	**15.6**
Lexical Errors	
Word choice	11.5
Word form	6.5
Informal usage	.3
Idiom error	.8
Pronoun error	2.9
Total Lexical Errors	**22.0**
Syntactic Errors	
Sentence structure	22.5
Run-ons	2.9
Fragments	1.8
Total Syntactic Errors	**27.2**
Mechanical	
Punctuation	6.8
Spelling	5.9
Total Mechanical Errors	**12.7**
Miscellaneous	.9
Total Number of Errors Marked: 5,707	

Source: Data taken from Ferris et al. 2000 research corpus.

Stage 2. Understand that different students may make distinct types of errors.

A danger with lists of "common" ESL errors, such as that in table 1, is that they may be overgeneralized to all students. The types of errors that ESL students may make in their writing may be influenced by many different factors, including the amount and nature of English language learning or expo-

sure to English that they have had; their current L2 proficiency (which may vary across lexical, syntactic, and morphological dimensions); and the influence of their particular
L1s. (In addition, of course, individual students will vary
across motivation levels, learning styles, time and energy
available, etc., but these types of individual variation patterns
also occur in native-English-speaking student writers.)

Students' English Language Learning Background

One of the most salient issues for teachers to consider is the
nature of students' prior exposure to English. For U.S. writing
instructors, it is important to recognize some crucial distinctions between international (visa) students and long-term U.S.
residents (whether immigrant or native born). As discussed
by Reid (1998a) and Ferris (1999b), international students are
more likely to be "eye" learners, meaning that their exposure
to English has been largely formal, delivered through books
and classroom instruction. Such students often have been educated with a strong English grammar foundation, have a good
grasp of key grammatical terms (e.g., parts of speech or lexical categories), and can articulate rules. It should not, however,
be assumed that this knowledge is always transferred accurately to student writing (or speech), as English language instruction in non–English speaking countries often focuses on
presenting linguistic information without many opportunities
to apply it to students' written or oral production. International students who have a good "textbook" grasp of the basics
of English grammar may benefit therefore from brief, focused
reviews of issues most salient for English writing and from opportunities to practice and apply principles of grammar to their
own writing. As this relates to error feedback, students who,
for instance, know what verbs are and understand the meanings and uses of different verb tenses may be able to take a code
such as "vt," marked above a verb tense error, and use it to access their previously learned knowledge to correct the error.

Permanent U.S. residents, on the other hand, are more likely
to be "ear" learners, meaning that their primary exposure to

English has been informal and oral (just as for native English speakers). Their acquired grasp of what "sounds" right may help them to select lexical items more accurately and to produce more idiomatically appropriate sentences. On the other hand, they may have little or no formal knowledge of grammatical terms or rules. Unfortunately for this group of students, most editing handbooks for ESL student writers assume the international student's base of knowledge, starting, for instance, with rules for how to select the correct verb tense in discourse or how to avoid errors in subject-verb agreement but overlooking the fact that some L2 students may not know the terms "verb," "tense," "subject," or "agreement."

It is therefore vital that teachers of L2 writers take time to ascertain what their students know about formal grammar before adopting or utilizing any sort of error-correction system. This can be done by means of a questionnaire and/or grammar-knowledge pretest at the beginning of the course (see app. 4B for samples). This will help teachers to develop a system of giving feedback that is responsive to students' knowledge, experience, and needs.

The Influence of Specific L1s

A second important way in which students may differ is in the influence of the L1 on their written production (and specifically on the errors they may make). Findings from contrastive analyses have suggested, for instance, that native speakers of Japanese may struggle with using English articles correctly, that Chinese speakers may have trouble with the English verb tense system, that Russian speakers may have difficulty with word order, and that Arabic and Spanish speakers may make errors in sentence boundaries. While the incidence of such error types will undoubtedly vary across individual speakers of particular L1s, such generalizations have practical implications for ESL composition teachers. For teachers of multilingual classes (as in many U.S. institutions), it is helpful to understand that not all students will make the same types of errors. Depending on the makeup of a particular class, teachers may wish to provide grammar and editing instruction individually or in small groups (rather than to the whole class) and may give students error feedback that helps them understand the target language structure by referencing the native language system. EFL instructors in homogeneous classes may find it beneficial, if they are not already native or fluent speakers of the students' L1, to investigate the similarities and differences between the syntactic and morphological systems of the L1 and English, to use this knowledge to assess students' particular strengths and weaknesses, and to design feedback and instruction that address these specific areas of need.

Differences in L2 Proficiency

Finally, teachers need to realize that differences in students' levels of L2 proficiency will affect both the number and type of errors that they make as well as their ability to process particular types of feedback. For an advanced international student or EFL learner, a cryptic code marked above an error, such as "pl," "vt," etc., might be sufficient to elicit an entire system of formally learned terms and rules. Students from the same L1, however, who are not very far along in either formal knowledge or language acquisition might be bewildered by such a mark or, if they do understand it, be unable to successfully correct the error. Brown (1994, 211–12) provides a helpful taxonomy of the stages of error recognition and ability to correct through which learners may pass. At the "random" and "emergent" stages, learners are completely or partially unsystematic in their uses of particular structures. An example of this might be an Arabic learner struggling with English spelling. This student's bewildered teacher may notice that the same word may be spelled three or four different ways in the same paper (including even correct spelling some of the time). When students are at these presystematic stages, they are typically not able to self-correct their errors or even to provide a correction when the error is pointed out. At more proficient levels, which Brown terms the "systematic" and "stabilization" stages, students' errors are more systematic, showing clearly what they know and what they have not completely mastered, and students are able to correct errors either on their own or when pointed out by teachers.

Understanding these stages of development has practical implications for providing error feedback. For students at lower proficiency levels, it may not be effective to simply locate an error (with or without a code or explanation) and ask the student to figure out the correct form. Instead, students may benefit from direct correction—the teacher providing the correct forms—and the opportunity to revise or recopy the text with the corrections inserted. This gives students needed input for acquisition, the "negative evidence" that some SLA researchers argue is necessary to prevent fossilization, and the opportunity to physically practice editing and correction of their own writing.

On the other hand, as students gain proficiency in English, it is important to give them feedback that will encourage, even require, them to analyze their errors and self-correct. While specific options and mechanisms for providing such indirect feedback are explained in detail later in this chapter, it is important at this point to remember both that students need a certain amount of knowledge of English to understand and utilize this type of correction and that teachers should be intentionally moving their student writers toward self-sufficiency and independence as editors.

Stage 3. Understand the need to prioritize error feedback for individual students.

Once teachers know, in general, what types of errors their students might make, they will need to make some decisions about which errors to mark. There are several criteria that teachers can consider in making this decision.

Global versus Local Errors

SLA and error-correction researchers have made a distinction between global errors—those that interfere with the overall message of the text—and local errors, which do not inhibit a reader's comprehension. The following two examples illustrate the difference.

(a) The tension was at its *pick.*
(b) Last summer I *go* to visit my grandmother in L.A.

In example (a), the lexical error (using *pick* instead of the intended word, which was *peak*) could completely confound a reader. In (b), on the other hand, the phrase *Last summer* places the sentence into the correct time frame, making the verb tense error (*go* instead of *went*) relatively harmless.

While the global/local distinction is intuitively appealing to teachers, it should be noted that the relative "globalness" of an error varies substantially according to the surrounding context of the error. It would be an overstatement, for instance, to say that all lexical errors are global and all verb tense errors are local, as can be seen in examples (c) and (d).

(c) San Francisco is a very *beauty* city.
(d) I *study* English for four hours every day.

Example (c) is a lexical error (word form), as a noun was used when the adjective form was required. Nonetheless, few readers would be confused about its meaning. The tense of the verb *study* in example (d) could be either correct or incorrect depending on the intended time frame of the statement, which might not be obvious from the surrounding context. Thus meaning (as to time frame) could be obscured if this is indeed a verb tense error, creating a global error that interferes with reader comprehension.

Frequent Errors

Another common way to prioritize error feedback is to focus on errors that individual students make frequently. There are two possible ways to approach this. One is to complete individualized error analyses for each student based on an early writing sample (see fig. 9 and app. 4C for samples). Based on this information, the teacher can provide each student with feedback targeted to her or his greatest areas of weakness. For instance, if a student appears to omit plural and possessive endings on nouns with relative frequency, the teacher may wish to focus on that error each time he or she provides feedback so that progress can be assessed. In addition, grammar instruction (whether for individuals, groups, or the entire class) can be designed based on these initial error analyses.

While early-term error analyses can be highly informative for the teacher (and are very much appreciated by student writers), they are likely too time-consuming for most teachers to do every time they read a set of student papers. In addition, students may very well make different types of errors on different assignments, either because they have made progress or because the text type they are producing calls for different types of constructions. Thus, the "problem areas" identified by analyses of diagnostic essays at the beginning of a course may not be the most significant issues on papers written later in the term. Teachers need, therefore, to perform on-the-spot error analysis each time they read a student text on which they are providing feedback. This can be as simple as reading the paper through quickly and identifying two or three frequent or serious patterns of error.

Structures Elicited by the Assignment or That Have Been Discussed in Class

In providing error feedback, teachers may also want to target grammatical, morphological, lexical, or mechanical issues related to in-class work or out-of-class reading. For instance, if students are writing a personal narrative and analyzing why an experience was important to them, it might be helpful to focus on the use of different verb tenses in discourse (past tense to describe the experience, present tense to describe what they think today about the incident, etc.) and to give students feedback about their success or lack thereof in negotiating these tense shifts. If students are working on an assignment in which they are required to incorporate the words of other authors, teachers may wish to give feedback about the mechanical and syntactic issues that arise in the use of paraphrase and quotation. Such feedback may be particularly effective if the teacher has already provided some instruction about those specific issues; feedback can then refer explicitly to this shared core of knowledge (see Reid 1994).

When Should Errors Be Corrected?

Timing of error correction is an important and sometimes controversial question in the teaching of both spoken and written English. In considering spoken English, teachers must walk a

---

ERROR-ANALYSIS SUMMARY FORM—DIAGNOSTIC ESSAY

Student name: _____

Error Type	Total Number of Errors and Percentage of Total	
Missing or unnecessary word	9/35	25.7 percent
Noun ending (plural or possessive) missing or incorrect	6/35	17.1 percent
Verb tense or form	6/35	17.1 percent
Article errors	4/35	11.4 percent
Punctuation	4/35	11.4 percent
Subject-verb agreement	3/35	8.6 percent
Word choice or form	2/35	5.7 percent
Sentence fragments	1/35	2.9 percent

Most serious errors to work on:

1. missing or unnecessary words
2. nouns (plurals, possessives, articles)
3. verbs (tense, subject-verb agreement)

fine line between lowering students' confidence and inhibiting their fluency and allowing errors in pronunciation, grammar, and vocabulary to "slip by" during class discussions or activities, perhaps misleading the students about what the correct forms really are. In teaching writing, many L1 and L2 composition theorists believe strongly that premature attention to error may short-circuit students' ability to think, compose, and revise their content. If teachers give too much error feedback early in the composing process (while students are still deciding what they want to say), students' further writing and revision become merely an exercise in proofreading rather than substantive thought (Sommers 1982; Zamel 1982, 1985). This danger is presumed to be especially salient to L2

Whole-Class Error Analysis

Based upon diagnostic essays written in one hour by 21 students (13 different L1s)

Error Type	Percentage of Total Errors
Nouns (plurals, possessives, or articles/determiners)	23.2 percent
Word choice or form	17.7 percent
Sentence structure problems: missing or unnecessary words	16.1 percent
Verb tense or form	13.5 percent
Punctuation	9.3 percent
Subject-verb agreement	8.3 percent
Spelling	7.0 percent
Sentence fragments/run-ons/word order/unclear sentences	3.7 percent
Pronoun wrong or unclear	.8 percent
Capitalization	.5 percent

Fig. 9. Sample error analyses for individual student and entire class

writers, who are only too well aware of their linguistic limitations and are thus more likely to focus on word- or sentence-level accuracy, to the detriment of the development of their ideas and improvement in written fluency.

However, recent studies have suggested that L2 student writers are both willing and able to benefit from simultaneous feedback on content and form on the same draft (e.g., Ashwell 2000; Fathman and Whalley 1990; Ferris 1995b, 1997). One argument for providing at least some grammar feedback on all marked student drafts is that *not* doing so misses the opportunity to provide feedback at a teachable moment. Since many L2 student writers have significant accuracy problems, they arguably need all the input they can get from their teachers. By refusing to provide such feedback until the very last draft, teachers can severely limit these opportunities for needed input. A compromise position is to provide general feedback about errors on preliminary drafts alongside comments about students' ideas and organization: *"As you revise this paper, be sure to pay attention to your verb tenses and to the placement of commas in your sentences. I've underlined several examples of each type of error on the first page of your essay."* On later drafts, the teacher can then shift the emphasis, providing more error feedback. A related issue is whether error feedback is useful or necessary on final versions of student papers (i.e., papers that will not be revised further). Studies suggest that students are unlikely to go back and correct errors marked by the teacher when they have already completed the project and received a grade and that such feedback, since students do not pay much attention to it, has little effect on their long-term development. Two possible pedagogical reasons for marking "final" drafts (perhaps by just highlighting or circling any remaining errors) are if students or instructors are charting types/numbers of errors on essay drafts throughout the semester or if students will have the option to revise the paper further for a portfolio submitted at the end of the course. Teachers should weigh the need for such "final" feedback against the very real possibility that students will ignore it.

How Should Teachers Provide Feedback?

The foregoing discussion of *which* errors to correct and *when* to correct them illustrates the range of options writing instructors have available to them in giving error feedback. These options are explained and illustrated in more detail in this section.

Option 1. Direct versus Indirect Feedback

As already noted in this chapter and in chapter 2, previous researchers have argued for the superiority of indirect feedback: indicating an error through circling, underlining, highlighting, or otherwise marking it at its location in a sentence, with or without a verbal rule reminder or an error code, and asking students to make corrections themselves. **Indirect feedback**, it is claimed, forces students to be more reflective and analytical about their errors than if they simply transcribed teacher corrections (**direct feedback**) into the next draft of their papers. Since students are required by indirect feedback to take more responsibility for their errors, they are likely to learn more from the process; to acquire the troublesome structures; and to make long-term progress in finding, correcting, and eventually avoiding errors.

While indirect feedback clearly has more potential to effect long-term student learning and improvement in written accuracy, there are at least three distinct circumstances in which teachers should consider the judicious inclusion of direct feedback: (1) when students are at beginning levels of English language proficiency; (2) when errors are "nontreatable"; and (3) when the teacher wishes to focus student attention on particular error patterns but not others. Figure 10 shows a portion of a student text containing both direct and indirect error feedback.

As already noted, students who are in the early stages of learning English may not have either the formal linguistic knowledge or the acquired competence to self-correct errors

It is possible for some immigrants to be ~~truely~~ happy in America. The
immigrants choose to come over here, they are dreaming of a new, a better
life in America. The immigrants treat America as their homeland. They
hope ~~can~~ find happiness in here, and most of them find it. Even they are
not ~~truely~~ happy ~~in~~ here, ~~but~~ they still being so strong to continue on the
life road.

Fig. 10. Student text portion with direct and indirect feedback.
Note: Only errors actually marked by the teacher are reproduced here.
(From Ferris et al. 2000 research corpus.)

even when their teachers point them out. Though it is unclear
whether direct correction combined with student revision or
recopying has a long-term effect on students' accuracy or their
overall acquisition of these structures, producing well-formed
sentences after receiving error correction at least gives them
input for acquisition; more importantly, it makes them aware
from the early stages of the need to edit and correct their work.
Absent such feedback, students may fossilize or overestimate
their knowledge and ability (Higgs and Clifford 1982; Scarcella 1996).

In addition to students' linguistic ability levels, the nature
of the errors being considered may argue for direct correction.
As already noted, a good proportion of the errors made by
developing ESL writers are "untreatable," meaning that there
is no rule to which students can turn to correct an error when
it is pointed out to them. The most common errors of this
type are errors in word choice and word form and awkward
or unidiomatic sentence structure. In such cases, it may be
more helpful for the teacher to suggest a different word or a
restatement of the sentence than to simply underline the word
or sentence and mark "wc" (word choice) or "ss" (sentence
structure). Again, students, by incorporating the corrections,
receive some input for acquisition and a reminder of the need
to select words and form sentences carefully.

Finally, direct correction may be appropriate if the teacher desires to give feedback about an error but wishes the student to primarily focus his or her attention on some other pattern of error. For instance, a hypothetical student may, in an 800-word essay, make three errors in verb tense or form but 15 errors with plural endings on nouns. The teacher may choose to simply correct the three verb errors while giving indirect feedback on the noun plural errors so that the student can really pay attention to her or his most serious problem on that paper (perhaps even checking a learner dictionary or studying the relevant sections of a grammar handbook on noun plurals). In sum, while indirect feedback may have the most potential to help student learning, direct feedback may have its legitimate role under certain circumstances.

Though direct feedback may be "easier" for the teacher and may please the students more in the short run (because it gives them the "right answer" and requires less effort on their part to make the corrections), overuse of direct feedback may lead to teacher "appropriation" of the student text. Both L1 and L2 researchers have warned teachers against using feedback to take over students' papers or "to put words into their mouths" (e.g., Brannon and Knoblauch 1982; Sommers 1982; Zamel 1985). A danger of direct feedback is that the teacher, in providing the correction rather than guiding the writer to do his or her own editing, will misinterpret the student's original intent about what he or she wanted to say. Figure 11 shows an example of (in this author's opinion) overzealous teacher correction and its impact on the student's paper. This is not to say that a teacher should abdicate responsibility for giving students helpful error feedback (see Reid 1994) but that direct feedback should be used with great care and only under the specific circumstances outlined earlier.

Option 2. Error Location versus Error Identification

Another decision teachers need to make in marking student papers is whether to simply **locate** the presence of an error (by circling it, highlighting it, or putting a checkmark in the

Example A: Student Draft with Teacher Feedback

_{adopts the new?}

An immigrant <u>practices their culture</u> within their community and as time go by
_{old}
the culture fades away.

Student Revision (next draft)

An immigrant practices their culture within their community and as time go by
the old culture fades away.

Analysis: The student ignored the first correction and incorporated the second.
Note that the first correction suggests a substantive change in the student's
original content. However, the teacher's inclusion of a question mark may have
indirectly given the student "permission" not to incorporate it.

Example B: Student Draft with Teacher Feedback

The first reason that immigrants can't be truly happy in America is because they
have to leave their country to start a new life. Every thing has to start over again.
~~Some people are forced to leave their country because of war or starvation.~~ It is
really sad for them to leave their country where they were born and lived for so
many years.

Student Revision (next draft)

The first reason that immigrants can't be truly happy in America is because they
have to leave their country to start a new life. Every thing has to start over again.
It is really sad for them to leave their country where they were born and lived for
so many years.

Analysis: In the earlier draft, the teacher simply crossed out an entire sentence
without any explanation as to why he felt that the sentence was a problem or
unnecessary. The student obediently deleted the sentence on her next draft. While
the teacher may have had a good pedagogical or rhetorical reason for the
suggestion to delete the sentence, this was not communicated to the student
through this feedback.

Fig. 11. Example of a teacher's direct feedback—and its results

margin) or to **identify** the types of errors that have been made,
using symbols, codes, or verbal comments (see option 4). The
primary argument for the former option (error location) is that
it places maximum responsibility on the student writer to
figure out both the nature of the problem and its solution.
There is growing evidence that in many cases, L2 students, just
like native speakers, rely on their own acquired knowledge of
the language to correct errors, only rarely relying on formally
learned terminology and rules to solve problems. For instance,

in the recent study by Ferris et al. (2000), students were able to correct errors that were located but not identified in 75 percent of the cases. More striking, when teachers coded errors *but used an incorrect code,* students were still able to successfully correct 62 percent of those errors, suggesting that, at least in those instances, they were relying on error location but not on (mis)identification to make the correction. Results of a follow-up experimental study by Ferris and Roberts (2001) similarly suggest that there is no significant advantage for error coding over simply underlining errors for students' ability to self-correct errors. The main reason to consider the latter option (identification) is that it provides more information to the students so that they can call upon their own prior knowledge or use resources such as grammar handbooks to understand or remember the rule and figure out how to apply it. Error identification can be cumbersome for the teacher and confusing for the student. It is also fraught with possibilities for misidentification. Many teachers feel a lot more confident about their ability to simply locate errors than to identify or label the particular type of error that has been made. On the other hand, error identification could be especially salient and appropriate if it refers specifically to an already defined error pattern on which the student is focusing and/or to errors that have been covered during in-class instruction. Under these circumstances, the teacher can label errors with firsthand confidence that students should be able to access a specific knowledge system in response to the labels.

Option 3. Larger versus Smaller Categories of Errors

If teachers are identifying or labeling specific patterns of student errors, another decision to be made is whether to use many **smaller categories** of error or several **larger categories**. The teachers in the Ferris et al. (2000) study (see table 1) opted for the former system, marking some 15 different errors (not including those in the "miscellaneous" category). ESL editing textbooks are about evenly split in their approach to this question. Popular texts by Lane and Lange (1993, 1999) and Raimes (1992) cover 15 and 21 error categories respectively, while texts by Fox (1992) and Ascher (1993) have only five to six chapters covering larger issues. For instance, teachers can mark and teach about "verb errors" (a large category) or break the treatment of verbs into several smaller categories, such as verb tense, verb form (which includes incorrect formation of the passive and errors related to modal usage), and subject-verb agreement. One can also talk about "noun errors" or about discrete errors in forming the plural or possessive, use of articles and other determiners, and pronoun-referent agreement. The argument for using smaller categories is that students can focus on a more limited range of forms and rules when learning about a specific error type. However, the use of 15 to 20 different terms or symbols to label errors may be overwhelming to teachers and students alike. Also, the distinctions among error categories are not always as precise as we may think. Teachers who are analyzing student errors or marking papers can have a hard time distinguishing between a verb tense and a verb form error or determining whether a lexical error results from problems with word choice or spelling. A final reason for considering the use of larger categories of error in marking and teaching is that often smaller errors have the same underlying cause. If a student omits an article or a plural marker when it is required, both errors may have the same root: a fundamental misunderstanding about the nature of nouns (count/noncount, abstract, collective, etc.). To summarize, the use of larger error categories may be preferable because it is easier for both teachers and students to deal with and because it may more accurately capture students' developing knowledge systems.

Option 4. Codes versus Symbols versus Verbal Comments

When teachers do choose to identify errors as part of indirect or direct correction, they must choose whether to use a set of

Error Type	Abbreviation/Code
Word choice	wc
Verb tense	vt
Verb form	vf
Word form	wf
Subject-verb agreement	sv
Article	art
Noun ending	n
Pronoun	pr
Run-on	ro
Fragment	frag
Punctuation	punc
Spelling	sp
Sentence structure	ss
Informal	inf
Idiom	id
Plural	pl

Fig. 12. Sample error codes. (From Ferris et al. 2000 research corpus.)

error codes (see fig. 12 for an example), to use **correction symbols** (as printers do), or to use **verbal cues** to identify errors. Figure 13 shows how the same error could be marked in six different ways depending on which strategy is used. The argument for using codes or symbols is speed and efficiency: teachers can write "vt" more quickly than "verb tense," and as they mark hundreds or even thousands of errors during a semester, this labor-saving device is not insignificant! On the other hand, teachers who use codes or symbols must take extreme care to mark consistently and to make certain that students understand what codes or symbols mean. Surveys of student reactions to teacher feedback have found that both L1 and L2 students resent cryptic codes or symbols that they do not understand (e.g., Ferris 1995b; Straub 1997). Some teachers, likewise, may find it more time consuming to learn, remember, and use a coding system consistently than to simply write the key word or term on a student's paper. Even when using complete words or phrases, though, the burden is on instructors to make sure that students understand what those references

---

*Original text portion: I never needed to worry about my parents because they knew everything and could go anywhere they **want.***

<u>Correction Options</u>

1. ***Direct correction:*** ... *could go anywhere they* ~~**want.**~~ **wanted**

2. ***Error location:*** ... *could go anywhere they* **<u>want</u>.**

3. ***Error code:*** ... *could go anywhere they* **<u>want</u>.** ^vt^

4. ***Error symbol:*** ... *could go anywhere they* **want** __^__

5. ***Verbal Cue:*** ... *could go anywhere they* **<u>want</u>.** ^tense^

6. ***Sample end comment:*** *As you revise, be sure to check your verbs to see if they need to be in past or present tense. I have underlined some examples of verb tense errors throughout your paper so that you can see what I mean.*

Fig. 13. Student text portion with different marking strategies

mean as well. Considering the example in figure 13, if a student doesn't grasp the meaning of "verb tense" or know which tense to select under what circumstances, it won't much matter whether the teacher writes "vt," inserts a ^, or writes "tense" in the margin.

Option 5. Textual Corrections versus End Notes

The final consideration facing teachers in marking errors is exactly *where* to place such marks. In most cases, the best place for error correction is at the specific **point of error**. However, a combination of error location (e.g., underlining) plus a **verbal summary** at the end of the paper or on a teacher feedback form may be very appropriate for advanced writers who are developing independent self-editing skills. In addition, if the teacher has implemented a program of tracking or charting student errors across drafts and assignments (see chap. 5), a summary form that indicates the major errors marked and perhaps how many of each type there are may be a key component of the program.

Other Considerations

One issue not already addressed will likely be highly familiar to the teacher of intermediate-level students, who are advanced enough in their L2 writing proficiency to attempt some ambitious sentence types and to utilize more challenging vocabulary but who in many cases do not have enough control over syntax and lexicon to execute complex sentences properly. Put more simply, what do teachers do with the "out-of-control" sentence that has so many errors that it's hard to know where to start—especially if the teacher is unable even to hazard a guess at the student's intended meaning? Figure 14 gives several examples of such sentences with possible options for giving feedback. One option is simply to give up—to underline or circle the sentence and put a giant question mark above or next to it or to say "I don't understand what

---

Original student text: *Study hard and work hard differences language and culture to adapt in social is a good thing to do for immigrant people to help them comfortably interact with diverse people and help them to deal with the discrimination.*

Actual Teacher Markings

(a) *Comment in margin:* **Rewrite this sentence. Break into two sentences.**

(b) *In-text codes/corrections:* Study hard and work hard differences
    language and culture to adapt in social is a good thing to do for
    immigrant people to help them comfortably interact with diverse
    people and help them to deal with the discrimination.

Alternatives

(a) *Rewrite the sentence:* **Studying hard and working hard to overcome differences between languages and cultures to adapt in society is . . .**

(b) *Eliminate the codes and marks on individual words and write the following comment:* **I'm not sure I understand this sentence. Can you rewrite it and try to make it clearer? You might try making it simpler by dividing it into two sentences.**

Fig. 14. Options for the "out-of-control" sentence

you mean here. Can you try to rewrite this sentence?" Another is to offer several suggestions about how to rewrite the problematic part of the sentence (or the whole sentence). Of course, this latter option is only available if the teacher has a clue about what the student writer is trying to say! In either case, giving fairly directive feedback in the form of asking the student to rewrite or offering a suggested rewrite is probably more effective than trying to make or elicit five or six micro-level corrections in the same sentence. Another potentially effective strategy, if feasible, is to ask the student writer to rephrase the sentence orally during a one-to-one writing conference.

Helping Students to Understand and Utilize Error Correction

As noted by Truscott (1996), teacher choices and behaviors are only half of the equation in grammar feedback. If students do not or will not attend to error feedback, do not understand such feedback when they do pay attention it, or do not know how to incorporate it into their writing or to apply it to future writing tasks, the teacher's efforts will be in vain. Thus, it is important for teachers (and students) to perceive error feedback as part of a larger strategy of building students' knowledge and strategy bases, not simply a "fix-it" list for a particular paper. Students need to be made aware of the need to improve their accuracy and build their own self-editing skills, and they need to see how the teacher's feedback fits into the development of these abilities (see chap. 5 for specific suggestions on raising students' awareness and motivating them). This, in turn, should motivate them to attend to teacher feedback when they receive it. Instructors can facilitate students' attention to accuracy by allowing (or requiring) students to rewrite texts after receiving error feedback, by allowing time in class for students both to ask questions and to actually go over their teacher-marked drafts and make corrections, by training them in error-correction strategies and pointing them to helpful resources (see chap. 5; Ferris 1995c; Reid 1998b), and by holding them accountable through the grading scheme for making a good-faith effort to utilize teacher feedback and to improve in their own editing skills and overall accuracy of their texts.

Conserving Energy and Avoiding Burnout

Writing teachers face a dilemma. They want to help their students to develop in every facet of their writing, including (and maybe even especially) their accuracy and control over standard written English. Yet, as I have noted elsewhere, responding to students' written errors can be time consuming and tedious. Worse, it does not always pay off in long-term student improvement (Ferris 1999a, 2). As an example, for a university ESL writing course I taught during the summer of 1998, I prepared individual error analyses for each of the 21 students, who had spent approximately 50 minutes in class writing diagnostic essays that ranged from about 400 to 800 words in length. Despite the fact that I am an experienced writing teacher and have done previous research involving error analysis (Ferris 1995c), it took me 11 hours to complete the task. I found it a valuable exercise, and my students truly appreciated my effort and felt that it helped them. But it was costly—and I certainly didn't keep it up for all of their subsequent papers!

This anecdote leads to a question that I am often asked when I give talks or conduct workshops on this topic: *How can teachers possibly manage the workload—especially bearing in mind that many teachers have more, and larger, writing classes than I do?* While there is unfortunately no "magic bullet" to make the process of giving error feedback incredibly fast or even moderately entertaining, a few suggestions can be offered to make the process of error feedback more efficient and satisfying.

1. *Do not feel that you must give written error feedback on every single paper students write.* Remember that teacher-student conferences (whether out of class or miniconferences during class), peer feedback, and self-evaluation are legitimate and valuable alternatives for various phases of the writing process, including the editing phase (see chap. 5; Ferris and Hedgcock 1998).

2. *Assess what your students know, find out what they want, and design your feedback strategies accordingly.* Once you have an idea of students' most common and serious errors, the level of formal knowledge of grammar that they possess, and their preferences with regard to error feedback, you can design a system of response that you can use consistently. As you and your students become comfortable with the process of feedback and revision, the provision of error feedback should become less stressful and more efficient.

3. *Set realistic goals for error feedback.* Error correction should *not* be seen as the means to eradicate all student errors but as the means to encourage gradual but consistent improvement in accuracy over time, acquisition and application of linguistic knowledge, and development of effective self-editing strategies.

4. *Make most of your feedback indirect, focused on error location rather than identification, and verbal (not tied to codes or symbols).* Once you have established your priorities for feedback, the quickest way to move through student papers is with highlighter in hand, locating key errors so that students can go back and attempt to self-correct and then adding a brief note about specific patterns of error to which students should attend.

5. *As time goes on, mark fewer errors and require the students to take increasing responsibility for their own progress.* This final strategy assumes that you are progressively training students to locate and identify errors, teaching them grammar rules they can use to address common errors, and giving them practice with sample and peers' texts in editing strategies (see chap. 5; Bates,

Lane, and Lange 1993; Ferris 1995c; Ferris and Hedgcock
1998; Reid 1998b).

Summary: Strategies for Giving Error Feedback

This discussion has covered a number of issues and options
for teachers to consider when providing error feedback to their
students. The list of suggestions in figure 15 summarizes these
issues and assumes that error correction in L2 writing classes

---

Before Giving Feedback
- Discover and consider what your students know—from prior language-
  learning experience and your own instruction—about specific grammar
  terms and rules and about editing strategies.
- Ask students what *they* prefer. All errors marked or only the major ones?
  Error identified or merely located? A set of symbols or verbal feedback?
- Decide on your specific strategies. Will you mark all errors or only the
  most frequent/serious? Will you use indirect or direct feedback or a
  combination of both? Will you use codes, symbols, or verbal comments?
  Will you make corrections on the paper itself or give feedback separately
  (at the end or on a feedback form)?

While Giving Feedback
- Read the student text through quickly—*without marking it*—to determine
  what the most serious issues are.
- Check yourself to see whether you are being clear (and legible!) and
  consistent with terms, symbols, and other markings.
- Be careful that you don't mislabel an error—if you're not certain what
  type of error it is, either look it up or just mark it without identifying it—
  and that you are focusing on *errors* rather than stylistic differences.

After Giving Feedback
- Be sure that students are clear about your error-marking strategies—that
  they understand especially codes/symbols and grammar terminology but
  also that they understand the principles of prioritizing and marking
  selectively.
- Give students time to ask you questions about their errors and to self-
  correct marked papers in class.
- Hold students accountable through the grading scheme for attempting to
  address your feedback.

Fig. 15. Summary of strategies for error feedback

should be planned and executed carefully by the teacher and be part of a larger strategy for building students' editing skills. For further reference, appendix 4D contains sample student papers with teacher markings and some commentary about the strengths and weaknesses of the error-correction strategies used, considering the ideas presented in this chapter.

In this chapter, I have provided an overview of many different questions and issues related to teacher correction of student errors. The fact that there are so many options to consider may be disappointing to some teachers, who may wish for a simple list of dos and don'ts that will work well for all students. But it is impossible and inappropriate to apply the same feedback strategies to all student populations and all situations. Only when instructors consider the needs, knowledge, and prior experience of students; make careful decisions about the goals and mechanics of error correction; and embed error feedback in a larger context of developing knowledge and building strategies that will improve student writing will such feedback have the desired effects on our students. Absent such careful decision making, teachers might as well accept Truscott's (1996, 1999) argument that grammar correction is ineffective and should be abolished.

Chapter 5

Beyond Error Correction: Teaching Grammar and Self-Editing Strategies to L2 Student Writers

It is clear that teacher correction is not the only way in which instructors can "treat" student error and help students to improve the overall accuracy of their texts. Even Truscott (1996, 1999), who opposes error correction in any form in L2 writing classes, admits that there may be a legitimate role for strategy training and grammar instruction as an alternative means of helping students to edit their writing. In this chapter, we will examine in some detail several important pedagogical issues and options related to treatment of student written error:

- the need to raise student awareness about the importance of editing;
- the need to give students training in self-editing strategies;
- the option of providing supplementary grammar instruction through the use of in-class minilessons, grammar handbooks, etc.;
- the option of utilizing peer- and self-editing workshops in conjunction with writing projects.

All four of these concerns, used in combination with thoughtful and consistent teacher feedback strategies, may help students to edit individual papers more effectively and to improve in accuracy over time. Included in the following discussion are a number of practical suggestions and tools that L2 writing instructors can use or adapt for their own specific contexts.

Helping Students Understand the Importance of Editing

As I noted in an earlier piece on this topic, "Though some teachers assume that all ESL students are obsessively concerned with grammar, to the detriment of developing and presenting their ideas, I have found that many of my students have little interest in and pay limited attention to editing their work. They find editing tedious or unimportant, or they have become overly dependent on teachers or tutors to correct their work for them" (Ferris 1995c, 18). This lack of interest, at least by some students, in focusing on editing may be attributed to two opposite reactions that L2 writers often receive from subject-matter instructors or even English writing instructors. On the one hand, subject-matter instructors may choose to focus only on students' ideas and mastery of course content, ignoring written language problems as unimportant to overall learning goals and excusing ESL writers' errors because of their language deficits compared with other students. It is certainly the right of instructors to privilege content over error in their feedback and grading schemes, and in many disciplines, this may be the most appropriate and humane approach. However, L2 writers need to understand that not all college/ university instructors may be as understanding of errors; that there may be universitywide writing or graduation assessments that require a threshold level of accuracy for students to pass; and that future employers, colleagues, and clients in the "real world" may expect their writing to be clear, accurate, and in accordance with the usage conventions of standard written English. L2 scholars such as Scarcella (1996) and Johns (1995) have written compellingly about the deficits L2 writers may face both in academia and in the workplace if they are not assisted with reaching basic standards of clarity and accuracy in writing (and in speech).

In addition to these external, instrumental issues, instructors should also point out that written errors can interfere with the comprehensibility of the message. In other words, students, as well as teachers, need to abandon the idea that there is a true distinction between "content" and "form." In fact, it is often a false dichotomy. Content determines form (e.g., if the author intends to tell a story that happened in the past, the verb tenses will follow appropriately from that content-based decision), but lack of accurate forms can obscure ideas. Fairly accessible examples of this include errors in word choice and in verb tense. Teachers can easily demonstrate this to students by creating a handout containing student sentences and/or essay excerpts in which student meaning is obscured or hidden altogether by errors in form (see app. 5B).

On the other hand, students may appear uninterested in developing competence in self-editing because of a lack of confidence or even fear that has been instilled in them by previous English and subject-matter instructors. L2 writers speak of receiving comments from teachers like "You really need to work on your grammar" or even "I will not read this paper until you correct the grammar mistakes." In surveys of student opinion about the importance of grammar feedback from writing instructors (e.g., Ferris and Roberts 2001; Rennie 2000), students typically respond that they feel they have serious grammar problems that impede the effectiveness of their writing and that they urgently need assistance from their teachers to produce accurate texts and to improve their linguistic control. In short, students feel overwhelmed by their own self-perceived lack of linguistic competence and by the negative feedback they may have received from previous instructors. The resulting lack of confidence may cause students to resist any attempt by teachers to help them develop self-editing strategies because they simply feel that they are not capable of finding and correcting their own errors.

While these two opposite extremes—students' lack of interest in editing because linguistic accuracy seems irrelevant and their lack of confidence that they can improve without extensive teacher intervention—can be daunting for instructors to combat, they are not insurmountable problems. As to the first belief, that grammar and accuracy are unimportant, teachers can raise student consciousness in the following ways.

1. They can demonstrate to students that many people (subject-matter instructors, prospective employers, instructors in graduate programs) do indeed feel strongly about written accuracy in student writing. Two possibilities for conveying this point convincingly are either to prepare a simple summary of published research on "error gravity" or to conduct a simple survey of different subject-matter faculty on one's own campus in order to get a sense of how they view error in L2 student writing. A perhaps even more effective option would be to interview or survey local employers in some of the students' chosen fields (e.g., business, computer science, engineering) to see how they would perceive inaccurate and unclear writing by prospective employees who are nonnative speakers of English. (See app. 5A for ideas on conducting such a survey.)

2. Teachers should also address the very salient issue of graduation writing requirements at their institutions, if such exist. In many U.S. universities (including the enormous California State University system), students must pass an upper-division writing assessment (essay examination, portfolio, or writing course) in order to receive their degrees. In many if not most cases, a grading rubric is utilized that includes linguistic control and the absence of serious or frequent errors as criteria that can affect passage (see fig. 16). Teachers should discuss such assessments and their grading criteria frankly with students, perhaps also showing them sample student texts that passed or failed the examinations primarily because of accuracy (or lack thereof). (See app. 5B for a sample exercise along these lines.)

3. To address both issues (irrelevance and confidence), teachers should provide students with a "reality check" based upon students' own writing at the beginning of the course. At the beginning of the class, most instructors

have access to one or both of the following samples of student writing: (a) a short, timed essay used by the institution to place students at the appropriate instructional level; (b) a diagnostic essay written in class during the first week of instruction. Writing teachers should exploit this information both to assess students so that they (teachers) can plan instruction appropriately and so that students can have an accurate sense of their abilities at the beginning of the term. In chapter 4 (fig. 9 and app. 4C), materials are provided to show how the teacher can do individual and class error analyses based upon diagnostic essays. Students should be given "individual report forms" (as in fig. 9) that give them a sense of what types of errors they make and their relative frequency. This is the more negative part of the "reality check."

Reviewers of my previous work and even student teachers I have supervised have expressed concern, even alarm, about the prospect of handing students such a black-and-white quantitative assessment of their language problems in writing. Wouldn't it offend students, showing them that we are only on an obsessive "error hunt" and that we don't care about the quality of their ideas? Wouldn't it frighten them, demotivate them, and torpedo their already shaky self-confidence? While my response to this is admittedly anecdotal and not empirical, I can assert that both my own students and the students of the graduate tutors whom I supervise have decidedly *not* taken offense at receiving such reports but on the contrary have expressed profound gratitude not only for the detailed and specific information that the reports provide but for the effort and attention they require on the part of their teacher. Students over and over have made comments like, "My English teachers always told me to work on my grammar, but this is the first time anyone has ever told me *exactly* what kinds of problems I have." If anything, I have found that providing this kind of attentive and concrete feedback creates a deep sense of trust in and respect for the writing teacher, a belief that she or he cares about their progress and is willing and able to take steps to help them. In response to this demonstrated commitment by the teacher, students will often work harder than they might have otherwise.

That said, however, I believe that the "reality check" can be profitably taken a step further and even promote student self-confidence. After reading students' placement or diagnostic essays, teachers can provide students with a two-step editing workshop that shows them how much they really can accomplish on their own (Ferris and Roberts 2001). In the first step, students are given their original diagnostic essay back and asked to find and correct as many errors as they can during a given period of time (say 20 minutes). For the second phase, the teacher highlights remaining errors that students didn't find. The students are given the paper again and asked to try to correct as many of the errors marked by the teacher as

---

6 Demonstrates clear competence in development, organization, and sentence structure
- Clearly addresses assignment with thoughtful thesis
- Is well organized and developed, using appropriate and effective details and analysis to support the thesis
- Demonstrates thorough understanding of the issues presented in the reading; documents sources of ideas and quotations
- Consistently uses language well; varied sentences and precise word choice
- Grammatical errors are rare and do not interfere with effectiveness of paper

5 Demonstrates competence in development, organization, and sentence structure but will have errors
- Addresses assignment with clear thesis
- Is generally well organized and developed, using effective details and analysis to support thesis
- Demonstrates competent understanding of the issues presented in the reading; documents sources of ideas and quotations
- Generally uses language well; varied sentences and clear and appropriate word choice
- Grammatical errors may occur throughout but are not serious and do not interfere with understanding

4 Demonstrates minimal competence in development, organization, and sentence structure but will probably have weaknesses in one or more areas
- Addresses assignment adequately with thesis, though it may be imprecisely worded or insufficiently focused
- Is adequately organized and developed, using details and analysis, though development may be thin at times
- Demonstrates adequate understanding of the issues presented in the reading; documents sources of ideas and quotations
- Uses language adequately; reasonable command of sentence structure and word choice
- May contain varied grammatical errors, but not to the point of interfering with understanding

↑   **Passing Paper**

↓   **Failing Paper**

3 Demonstrates developing competence in writing but remains flawed in development, organization, and/or language
- May not respond adequately to the topic or be sufficiently focused
- May not be adequately organized or developed; may be illogical or have insufficient or inappropriate support for thesis
- May demonstrate lack of understanding of the issues presented in the reading; may fail to document sources of ideas or quotations
- May have an accumulation of errors in sentence structure and word choice and form
- May have an accumulation of grammatical errors; errors may interfere with understanding

2 Demonstrates serious problems in writing
- Does not deal adequately with topic; may be off the point, unclear, or poorly focused
- May have serious problems with organization and development, use little or no detail, or have irrelevant specifics or unsupported generalizations
- May demonstrate serious misunderstanding of the issues presented in the reading; may fail to document sources of ideas or quotations
- May have serious and frequent errors in sentence structure and word choice and form
- May have an accumulation of serious grammatical errors that interfere with understanding

1 Demonstrates incompetence in writing
- May be unfocused, confusing, or incoherent; may completely misunderstand the issues presented in the reading
- May be severely underdeveloped
- May contain severe and persistent errors that interfere with understanding

Fig. 16. Sample ESL grading criteria for a university writing class. (From Department of English, California State University, Sacramento.)

possible. The teacher then analyzes the students' success ratios in finding and correcting errors unassisted and after feedback and returns the papers with an "editing report form." (See app. 5C for procedures and a sample report form; also see fig. 9.)

Though this editing process will require effort by both teacher and students and will consume some precious class time, it can have a powerful effect on student self-confidence. Students can observe firsthand that they really can self-edit their papers with fairly minimal teacher feedback (or even no feedback at all). This not only will help them to approach timed writing assessments with more confidence but will also serve as a powerful argument for the use of indirect (rather than direct) feedback by the teacher. This exercise will clearly demonstrate for students that they really can fend for themselves, at least to some extent, without excessive intervention by the teacher. Such a demonstration will likely be far more convincing than any explanation by the teacher about feedback procedures and may go a long way toward relieving student anxiety and frustration.

4. That said, teachers also should provide verbal explanations of their feedback and error-treatment philosophies and procedures. Student survey research on teacher feedback has clearly indicated that students are aware of (or can be convinced of) the need for teacher response to focus on issues other than grammar or error, as long as error is *one* of the concerns of teacher feedback (Brice and Newman 2000; Ferris 1995b; Ferris and Roberts 2001; Hedgcock and Lefkowitz 1994; Rennie 2000). Students also appear to understand, when it is presented reasonably to them, that it is to their benefit to learn to find and correct their own errors and that indirect teacher feedback can help them to do that as well as or better than direct feedback (Brice and Newman 2000; Ferris and Roberts 2001; Rennie, 2000). Thus, teachers should explain from the outset *how and why* they will give feedback (on all aspects of writing, including errors) and

should periodically remind students of their philosophies and practices (Brice and Newman 2000). At the same time, they should balance their own beliefs with what students tell them about their needs and preferences for error feedback, considering student views as well (Brice and Newman 2000; Ferris 1995b, 1997; Reid 1998b).

In sum, there are several reasons why students may be reluctant to engage in self-editing tasks, and there are a number of steps teachers can take to combat the inertia, whether it stems from over- or under-confidence. It is important to think through approaches to raising students' consciousness and motivation about editing so that students will "buy into" teacher feedback and other error-treatment strategies but more significantly so that students will take the need for accuracy and editing seriously enough to put forth the considerable effort that long-term improvement will undoubtedly require.

Training Students in Self-Editing Strategies

Though there is considerable disagreement as to whether error feedback is helpful and whether grammar instruction benefits student writers, experts in L2 writing are unanimous that students need to develop self-editing skills and that classroom strategy training may well be useful to them (e.g., Bates, Lane, and Lange 1993; Ferris 1995a, 1995c, 1999b; Ferris and Hedgcock 1998; James 1998; Reid 1998b; Truscott 1999). Strategy training for developing self-editing ability should include the following components.

Helping Students Become Aware of Their Most Pervasive Patterns of Error

As discussed in chapter 4 (see especially fig. 9 and app. 4C) and in the previous section, a detailed, comprehensive error analysis by the teacher can be an invaluable tool not only for the instructor but for individual student writers, giving them a clear-cut numerical sense of what their major issues are. In addition to this, if students have had previous L2 writing and grammar instruction, they may well have some fairly specific ideas about their areas of weakness. In a study by Ferris and Roberts (2001), 72 university ESL writers were asked to identify from a list what their major grammar problems were, according to both their own assessment and/or what they had been told by previous English teachers. Their responses matched up identically with the patterns of error they produced in diagnostic essays written during the first week of the semester.

Educating Students about Principles of Second Language Acquisition and Successful Self-Editing

Students may, either from their own intuitions or from feedback from previous instructors, feel that all error is "bad" and that it is both necessary and possible to strive for error-free writing in a short period of time. They need to be informed of research that indicates that error is a natural part of language acquisition and that it may even signal progress rather than deficiency, that steady improvement and not perfection is the appropriate goal, and that language acquisition takes time and requires both effort and patience. Figure 17 shows six understandable principles of editing that I have found helpful in presenting these ideas to college-level ESL writers.

Sharing Specific Editing Strategies

The strategies listed in figure 17 also give students specific suggestions about editing. The first, and perhaps the most crucial, is to remind students that they do need to make time for the editing phase, whether they are writing a paper outside of class or in a timed essay exam. Other ideas include reading the paper aloud (if possible); reading it from back to front (breaking the flow of ideas in this way sometimes helps writers to attend to language details rather than content); asking a friend to proofread the paper; and using the dictionary,

Definition of editing: Looking over a paper you have already written to find and correct any errors in grammar, vocabulary, punctuation, or mechanics (spelling or capitalization)

GENERAL ADVICE (for any paper)

1. Leave **plenty of time** to read over your papers. After you have written a paper, put it aside for an hour or two (even a day or two). Print out or photocopy your draft and go over it with a pen or highlighter. Looking at your paper again with a clear mind will help you to find errors.

2. **Read your paper aloud.** This will help you to notice errors you might miss if you were reading silently and quickly. You might also try starting from the end of your paper and reading "backwards"—read the last sentence, then the one before it, etc.

3. If you are using a computer, **run a spell-check** to catch any misspellings or typos. **But be careful!** The computer won't mark any mistakes that are "real" English words (e.g., "their" instead of "there"). You will still need to proofread your paper yourself after you spell-check. Also, **do not rely on the grammar checker!** It is designed for native speakers and is not programmed to catch errors made by ESL students.

4. **Ask a friend to read your paper** and see if he or she notices any problems. But be careful—if your friend always corrects your errors, you won't learn how to find and correct problems by yourself. Also, be sure to also read the paper yourself—remember, your friend's advice could be wrong! (Even native speakers of English make grammar mistakes!)

5. Be aware of your own **individual error patterns** (see error-analysis form from your diagnostic essay) and check your papers carefully for those problems. For instance, if you know you forget noun endings a lot, go through the paper and check all the nouns (a highlighter always helps!). If you're not sure of a particular grammar rule, check a textbook or ask a teacher, tutor, or friend for help.

6. **Be patient.** Learning grammar and writing skills in a second language takes time and effort. Don't expect to produce "perfect" papers right away! Keep track of your errors and work toward making fewer of them with each draft or new paper. Remember that you do *not* have to have a perfect, error-free paper to pass this class!

Fig. 17. Strategies for self-editing

grammar handbooks, and computer spell-check and gram-mar-check programs wisely.

Training Students to Make Focused Passes
through a Text to Look at Specific Issues

My junior-high-age daughter is an advanced student of Span-ish as a second language. She recently expressed frustration that she makes a lot of errors in verb tenses when she writes compositions in Spanish. I sat down with her and her most recent draft of a paper and had her read it aloud, focusing only on the individual verbs. It turned out that there were only two sentences in her composition in which she had to worry about her verb tenses. With one sentence, she explained to me why the imperfect (rather than the simple past tense) was appro-priate and checked in her Spanish grammar book to see what the appropriate imperfect verb form was. In the second sen-tence, as I read it aloud to her, she heard that she had (erro-neously) used the simple past tense and was able to make the correction. She found the whole issue of Spanish verb tenses much less overwhelming when she examined them verb by verb and realized that there were only two cases she really needed to think about and that she could solve her problem by think-ing through what she had learned about verb tenses and check-ing forms in her Spanish book. In English writing (her first language), she is prone to comma splice errors, but as I have consistently reminded her to check for them over the past couple of years, she has greatly reduced the frequency of this error and can monitor for it when reminded.

With ESL writers, as with my daughter, the task of self-editing feels much more manageable when students can prior-itize ("I have trouble with articles and noun plurals but almost never with verb tenses, so I should check all my nouns care-fully but not worry about the verbs") and make careful passes through a completed text to examine a particular issue. They can be easily trained to do this by means of exercises such as the one shown in figure 18. It is helpful to do this type of ed-iting exercise first through a whole-class demonstration with

Verb Tense Editing Exercise

Read through the student essay and highlight or underline every verb or verb phrase. Some of the verbs have errors in tense. Circle the verbs you think have tense errors. Be prepared to explain to a partner why you think those verbs are incorrect while the others are correct.

> Children start learning how to write more from their parents than any other people. Therefore, parents are big influences on their kids. Children need their parents' encouragement. They also need a good environment to study in.
> When I was a child, my parents spent their spare time helping me read newspapers. My father encouraged me to read by telling me that he wanted me to read all news. My father expected me to be good in school. He never forced me to read or write, but he always said, "Spending your spare time in reading and writing will help your knowledge improve." My father wanted to take me to the library every weekend. However, we lived in a poor country with few books and no public libraries. Therefore, my father took me to a small bookstore which was far away from my home. I started reading the Saigon news. Six months later, I realized that my reading had improve. This time I read by myself, and I don't wait until my father asked me to read. I volunteered to read for my father. One day he said, "Compared to other kids who are the same age as you, you are a very good kid because you are my good son." I was very happy when he said "because you are my good son." I promise myself that I would do whatever my father expected me to do. The way my parents influence me is very simple, but it's very important for me to take his advice to improve my reading.
> In my experience, having a good place to study is very important. For myself, my father had create a good environment for me even though we live in a tiny house. He make a small table for me to read and write in a corner of the house. He said, "This is your private place to study. You can read and write whatever you feel like." My father not only made the table, but he also bought me some short stories to read.
> These are the ways my parents influence my reading and writing. I believe it is unnecessary to have parents who have a high level of education. It is important how parents encourage their children.

Fig. 18. Editing for specific forms or error types. *Note:* This exercise assumes that students have had prior experience with identifying verbs and understanding the forms and usages of the simple present, simple past, present perfect, and past perfect tenses. (Source of student essay: Ferris and Roberts 2001 research corpus. Used with permission.)

a sample student text (using an overhead transparency and/or student handouts). Then students can do peer-editing activities (discussed later in the chapter) in which they look only for specific structures to see if there are any problems; they then can progress to self-editing their own texts for problems with particular target items. Figure 19 shows an example of a class-, peer-, and self-editing workshop that I have used with ESL college writers at several different levels of instruction.

Exercise 1: Understanding Different Verb Tenses

Look at this excerpt from the essay "Robo Teacher" (Kastorf 1993). For each highlighted verb, complete the chart below. The first one is done for you.

1. I once **heard** my aunt, herself a teacher, speculate on why educators **refuse** to use computers to their full capacity. 2. She **said** many teachers **are** afraid that they would be eventually replaced by teaching machines.
3. This idea **interested** me, so over the years I **have watched** teachers to decide whether or not they could be replaced by robots. 4. My conclusion **is** that the best teachers could never possibly be replaced by machines, but to save money, the mediocre ones could be—in fact, should be—replaced.

Verb (sentence number)	Tense	Explanation
heard (1)	**past**	**Talks about a one-time event (see the time signal "once")**
refuse (1)		
said (2)		
are (2)		
interested (3)		
have watched (3)		
is (4)		

Exercise 2: Analyzing a Classmate's Verb Tense Usage

Exchange essays with a partner, using the paper you wrote at the beginning of this chapter or another piece of writing you have done recently. With a pencil, circle each example you find of **present tense, past tense,** or **present perfect tense** (ignore other verb forms and tenses for now). Then complete the chart below just as you did in Exercise 1. **If you find any errors in verb tense, do NOT correct them. (You may discuss them with your partner in a few minutes.)**

Verb	Tense	Explanation

Verb	Tense	Explanation

After you have completed the chart, spend a few minutes discussing it with your partner. See if the two of you can agree on: (a) the tense of each verb you circled; (b) an explanation for why that tense was used in that sentence. If you have any questions, discuss them with your teacher.

Exercise 3: Editing Your Own Writing

Using the information from your partner's chart (Exercise 2) and your follow-up discussion, go through your essay and make any corrections to verb tense (present, past, or present perfect) that you think are necessary.

Fig. 19. Class-, peer-, and self-editing workshop

Encouraging Students to Track Their Progress in Self-Editing

As already noted, L2 writers may feel overwhelmed and intimidated by the challenge of reducing error frequencies and improving the overall accuracy and clarity of their writing. The consistent use of error logs or charts is one suggested mechanism for helping students to track and measure their progress (Ferris 1995a, 1995c; Ferris and Hedgcock 1998; Hendrickson 1980; Lalande 1982; Lane and Lange 1999). As noted in chapter 2, there has been little research done on the effectiveness of error logs as a pedagogical device, but the few studies that have been completed suggest that they are at least potentially beneficial consciousness-raising tools. In a qualitative case study that drew from a large quantitative text-analysis project (Ferris et al. 2000; Komura 2000), Roberts (1999) identified a number of logistical problems associated with the error logs used in that particular study and suggested a number of ways that the process could have been improved, including better explanation and integration of the error logs into classroom procedures and using fewer error categories and codes (see fig. 20).

A possible danger with using error logs is that students will focus on raw numbers alone and become either discouraged or complacent. To avoid these extremes, instructors need to discuss several issues with students. (1) As students improve in fluency and their texts become longer, they may make more total errors. Thus, students need to think in terms of **error-frequency ratios** (total errors divided by total numbers of words) rather than simple error counts. (2) Various written genres may elicit different linguistic structures. Thus, students may, for example, have few problems in producing correct verb tenses in a personal narrative that requires mainly the use of commonly used tenses such as simple present, simple past, and present perfect. However, if asked to produce a text about a hypothetical situation in the future ("Imagine that it is the year 2050. What do you think the world would be like?"), they

Verb errors	All errors in verb tense or form, including relevant subject-verb agreement errors
Noun ending errors	Plural or possessive ending incorrect, omitted, or unnecessary; includes relevant subject-verb agreement errors
Article errors	Article or other determiner incorrect, omitted, or unnecessary
Wrong word	All specific lexical errors in word choice or word form, including preposition and pronoun errors. Spelling errors only included if the (apparent) misspelling resulted in an actual English word.
Sentence structure	Errors in sentence/clause boundaries (run-ons, fragments, comma splices), word order, omitted words or phrases, unnecessary words or phrases; other unidiomatic sentence construction

Fig. 20. Description of major error categories. (From Ferris and Roberts 2001; see also Ferris and Helt 2000.)

may make many verb errors as they struggle with unfamiliar future and conditional forms. Looking at error-log counts, they could be alarmed by their apparent regression in their control of verb tenses without taking into account the complexity of the verb tenses called for by the writing task. In contrast, if a subsequent writing task again elicits simpler verb tenses, students may feel that they have made dramatic "improvements" when in fact problems remain in some areas. (3) Students also need to understand that steady overall progress in second language acquisition may lead to a more sophisticated writing style, resulting in student writers taking greater risks with both lexical choice and syntactic variety—and possibly an increase in error frequency. It is easier to avoid errors when one produces simple, one-clause constructions with no subordination, use of prepositional phrases and other adverbials, relative clause constructions, etc. Since instructors certainly do not want to discourage students from taking risks and developing a more mature writing style, they need to help students see that relative error frequencies are certainly not the only measure of high-quality writing. However, as a test-taking strategy, they may wish to suggest that students save "risky" uses of vocabulary and complex sentence structure for out-of-class multiple-drafting situations (when they can get feedback and revise) or for journal entries (when the goal is fluency and low-risk self-expression) rather than in-class essay examinations.

Teaching Students How to Edit under Time Pressure

An unfortunate reality for many ESL college students in the United States is that they must pass timed essay examinations in order to pass their English classes and/or to graduate. Though there are many reasons why L2 writers struggle to succeed in these situations (including difficulties with addressing the writing task adequately, developing a topic and providing effective support, and organizing an essay successfully), the lack of linguistic accuracy that results when students have to produce written texts under stress (because of the high stakes)

SUGGESTED SCHEDULE

10 min.: Go over the question. Highlight key words and instructions.

10–15 min.: Plan your essay. Write a thesis statement and a brief outline of your supporting points, including information from the readings.

75 min.: Write your essay. Check your outline as you go along. Plan to write at least four to six well-developed paragraphs (10–15 minutes per paragraph).

20 min.: Proofread and edit your essay. Watch out for:
- missing words;
- words you're not sure about;
- missing noun or verb endings;
- punctuation errors, especially with quotations;
- verb tense problems.

Fig. 21. Sample time-management plan for in-class essay exam. *Note:* The following schedule was suggested for a two-hour final examination in which students responded to an essay prompt derived from two readings they had previously completed and to which they were allowed to refer during the exam.

and under time pressure is clearly a major contributing factor to student failure in many contexts.

Thus, an important part of helping students develop successful editing strategies is to talk with them about what they can do when they have limited time and resources to proofread and edit their papers. To do this, I suggest the following process.

- Remind students that editing issues are included in the grading criteria for the exam and that they need to take them seriously.
- Talk with students about how they can/should manage their time during the exam (see fig. 21 for an example).
- Be sure that each student is aware of at least two or three individual patterns of error that he or she should monitor for when time is limited.
- Give them a few general pieces of advice (based upon common ESL writing errors) that they can remember (see figs. 21 and 22).

Instructions: You will have exactly 20 minutes to proofread and edit the attached student essay. Imagine that you have written it during an exam and that you are now checking for errors before you turn it in. Read through the paper quickly, using the questions below as a guide. Mark and suggest a correction for any errors you find.

- Are there any spelling errors?
- Are there any words missing in the sentences?
- Are there any words used incorrectly? Can you suggest a better word or word form?
- Look at the nouns. Do they have the right singular or plural endings? Is an article needed? Has the right article been used?
- Look at the verbs. Do the verb endings agree with the subjects? Are the verbs in the right tense?
- Look at the punctuation. Do you see any problems with commas, periods, semicolons, quotation marks, etc.?

Fig. 22. Editing under time pressure exercise

- Consider having them do "practice" timed editing activities (see fig. 22) on either sample student essays or on a draft of something they have already written.
- Build their proofreading and editing abilities throughout the course through the use of in-class editing workshops even for papers written out of class (see fig. 23). You can give them a personalized report afterward about their success ratios (as in fig. 23).

Providing In-Class or Individualized Grammar Support

Another component integral to the treatment of error in L2 writing classes is focused grammar instruction. There is a fair amount of disagreement among second language acquisition researchers and writing experts (both in L1 and L2) as to whether or not classroom instruction in grammar, vocabulary, and other formal aspects of language is effective in building target language competence and improving the accuracy and

Instructions: Using the codes listed below, I have marked your errors in the five categories listed. You will have exactly 20 minutes to go through your paper and try to make as many corrections as you can, using the codes to help you understand what the error is.

Code	Meaning
v	error in verb tense or form
ne	noun ending (plural or possessive) missing or unnecessary
art	article or other determiner missing, unnecessary, or incorrectly used
ww	wrong word or word form
ss	sentence structure: missing or unnecessary words; wrong word order; run-ons; sentence fragments

STUDENT REPORT FORM: IN-CLASS EDITING EXERCISE

Student Name: _____

Error Type	Number of Errors	Number You Corrected
Verb tense/form incorrect		
Noun endings missing, unnecessary, or incorrect		
Articles/determiners missing, unnecessary, or incorrect		
Word choice or word form incorrect		
Sentence structure: missing or unnecessary words, word order, fragments, run-ons, comma splices		
Totals		

Fig. 23. Sample in-class editing exercise

clarity of linguistic output (Atwell 1998; Byrd and Reid 1998; Doughty and Williams 1998; Ferris 1995c; Ferris and Hedgcock 1998; James 1998; Weaver 1996). To the degree that there is consensus on the teaching of grammar in writing classes, experts agree that it should have the following characteristics.

- It should consist of brief minilessons, rather than extensive grammar presentations.
- Lessons should be narrowly focused (e.g., on the contrast between simple past and past perfect tenses rather than on all 12 English verb tense/aspect combinations).
- Topics for minilessons should be selected based upon teacher (and perhaps student) analysis of class needs (as determined by detailed examination of student writing samples and/or by objective grammar/editing tests).
- Minilessons should always be explicitly connected to the students' own ongoing writing projects.
- Minilessons might include any or all of the following components: (1) "discovery" exercises (text analysis designed so that students can examine how the target language structures naturally occur in authentic discourse); (2) deductive presentation of key terms and rules with ample illustrations (sample sentences and text portions); (3) editing exercises in which students find, label, and suggest corrections for errors with the target construction; (4) application activities in which students examine their own writing or the writing of their peers for correct and incorrect uses of the particular structure being studied.
- Because student needs in a given class may be varied, the teacher may present minilessons to the entire class, to small groups within the class, or even in one-on-one conferences with individual students.

A Sample Minilesson Sequence

In the two recent studies that my colleagues and I completed with immigrant student writers two semesters below college level (Ferris et al. 2000; Chaney 1999; Ferris and Helt 2000; Ferris and Roberts 2001; Komura 1999; Roberts 1999), we found that many of the student writers had problems with selection and/or formation of appropriate verb tenses, other verb form issues (e.g., use of the passive voice), and subject-verb agreement. In this setting or in others like it, several different whole-class minilessons on verb tense and form might

be beneficial. The sample sequence shown in appendix 5D illustrates a minilesson that focuses students on tense shifts in
written discourse between past and present tense. It assumes
that students have a working knowledge of the term "verb"
and that they have been introduced to the form, meaning, and
use of simple past and simple present tenses. In Step 1, students are given a brief explanation of the need to maintain
consistency in verb tense usage and to shift tenses appropriately, sometimes using time markers. A brief sample paragraph
is used to illustrate these concepts. In Step 2, a discovery
exercise, students examine the verb tense usage in an excerpt
from an authentic text, simply labeling highlighted verb phrases
as being either in past or present time, identifying the reasons
for tense shifts, and underlining any time markers they find.
They then extend this analysis to their own writing in Step 3,
again simply analyzing tense usage (as opposed to editing for
errors, though this may also happen in the course of the exercise). In Steps 4 and 5, they edit verb tense errors (past vs.
present tense errors only) first in individual sentences and
then in a student essay excerpt. The follow-ups to this lesson
are lessons on use of the present and past perfect and then opportunities to pull the information together by peer- and self-
editing texts for errors in verb tense usage.

The amount of time given to this sequence or others like it
could vary depending on the needs of the student writers. If
students are already well acquainted with the terminology
and rules, they could spend most of their time applying their
knowledge through focused passes at sample student texts,
peers' writing, and their own papers. If they have had little
or no grammar instruction before, the teacher could spend
additional time going over the specifications of the various
tenses and on discovery activities. Also, some of the practice
exercises could be done as homework assignments with answer keys attached for self-study.

Minilessons for "Untreatable" Errors

The verb tense lesson sequence discussed above is reasonably
straightforward. Almost any reputable ESL grammar book will

contain ample information for teachers to refer to in preparing brief explanations and practice exercises for their students. But what are teachers to do about the very pervasive and troubling error types—such as word choice and unidiomatic sentence structure—that have no rules students can apply to find, diagnose, and correct such errors and to avoid them in the future? In such cases, instructors can design minilessons that highlight strategies and resources students can use to avoid or monitor for such errors if they are prone to making them. Appendix 5E shows such a sequence for word choice errors. It includes a brief definition with examples of "word choice errors" and then goes on to illustrate five "sources" of word choice errors (ranging from carelessness in proofreading to phonological interference). Practice exercises ask students to find word choice errors, identify what caused them, and suggest possible corrections. An "editing guide" provides suggestions about strategies for avoiding word choice errors in the students' own writing.

Selecting and Adapting Text Models for Minilessons

As the earlier discussion illustrates, the use of both published texts and sample student texts can be very helpful in designing grammar minilessons for the writing class. (They are valuable for illustrating many writing issues other than grammar, as well.) As with many other aspects of teaching, selection of text models for classroom instruction is not as simple as it may appear. For discovery activities that utilize authentic texts (i.e., not designed especially for the language class), if at all possible, I like to use texts with which students are already familiar, for instance, a reading from a class textbook that they have already covered. Prior knowledge of the content of the text helps students to process it better and thus to focus well on the structure they are examining as the goal of the minilesson. If no reading that has already been used illustrates the structure clearly and adequately, another possible source is other ESL reading or writing textbooks with texts at appropriate levels of difficulty. The text (or text portion) should be short and accessible, with vocabulary and concepts not so abstract or unfamiliar that meaning will impede students' ability to isolate the target constructions. Remember that the purpose of discovery exercises is to examine how the structure occurs naturally in authentic texts, not to build students' reading comprehension skills.

Developing discovery or editing exercises based upon sample student texts can be even more challenging. I have found several principles to be helpful in this process.

- Do not use texts written by students in the current class, as it may embarrass them or shake their confidence. Instead, with students' permission, make copies of student papers in a current class for use in a future class at the same or a similar level. It can also be valuable to trade student models with other instructors who teach students at equivalent levels of proficiency.
- Avoid student models that have numerous instances of word choice and sentence structure errors that render major portions of the text incomprehensible. Even if you are focusing on a very specific issue such as the use of articles, it can be very distracting to sort through confusing prose to find the target construction.
- If the minilesson is focusing on one particular issue or contrast, consider correcting yourself other errors in the text that are unrelated to the main point of the lesson. This will help students to focus only on the structures relevant to that day's lesson. Alternatively, you can highlight or underline only the structures or errors you want students to analyze, as in appendix 5D, Steps 2 and 4, building their skills up to where they examine a text independent of such assistance (as in Step 5).
- Once you have helped students learn to isolate various error types through separate passes through a text, you may want to select a student text containing errors in several major, common categories so that they can learn to edit papers for different problems, especially under time pressure (see instructions in figs. 22 and 23 as examples).

Additional Resources for Self-Study

Teachers may find that student writing problems are fairly scattered and idiosyncratic and/or that some students may need additional information and practice on particular language structures. It can be helpful to make various resources available to students, including ESL editing handbooks (e.g., Ascher 1993; Fox 1992; Lane and Lange 1999; Peterson and Hagen 1999; Raimes 1992); general-purpose ESL grammar textbook series; learner dictionaries; interactive software programs; and packets of teacher-created handouts and exercises, especially with sample student writing that features multiple examples of particular error types for students to examine and practice editing. Depending on resources available to teachers and students, teachers can make such materials available in a program library or computer lab, for purchase in the campus bookstore, or on a class website. Over the course of the semester, as I have gotten to know the needs of individual student writers, I have found it helpful to give them individual grammar/editing assignments based upon a required class editing handbook and/or a packet of materials I have created myself.

Once teachers have selected additional resources and arranged to make them available to students, it can be productive to spend a bit of class time discussing how to use such tools effectively. For instance, the teacher can design exercises around a learner dictionary to help students understand how to use noun plurals and articles accurately by checking whether a noun is count or noncount. Student writers should also receive instruction (and warnings) about the uses and abuses of spell-check and grammar-check tools included with commercial word-processing programs (see Ferris and Hedgcock 1998, chap. 9, for sample lessons on these issues).

Under no circumstance should a writing class be turned primarily into a grammar class, as there are many other issues besides linguistic accuracy that are critical to students' writing development. Still, focused grammar instruction that targets specific writing problems and simultaneously teaches rules and editing strategies can be a key aspect of error treatment in the writing class. When it is combined with teacher feedback that is selective and consistent and with editing-strategy training, it can give students the tools to eventually diagnose and solve their own writing problems.

Utilizing Peer- and Self-Editing Workshops in the L2 Writing Class

In the preceding discussion, a number of passing references are made to peer- and self-editing activities as key components of strategy training and grammar minilessons. However, like teacher feedback and in-class grammar instruction, the inclusion of such activities is not without controversy in the L2 writing literature. Many writing instructors, even if they utilize peer-response activities while students are drafting and revising the content of their texts, are leery of using peer-response sessions at the editing phase of the writing process. The argument against peer response is simple: It appears (often to both students and teachers) to be "the blind leading the blind" (Berger 1990; Leki 1990; Zhang 1995). L2 student writers by definition lack nativelike control of linguistic structures, so how can they possibly be competent enough to give helpful error feedback to their peers?

While this argument is certainly compelling in and of itself, there are, in my opinion, several good reasons for implementing peer-editing workshops as part of an overall error-treatment process, and there are several ways to limit and mitigate potential problems that may arise. The primary reason for using peer editing as a technique should not be so that the peer editor can necessarily "fix" all of the problems in his or her partner's paper but so that *readers* (the editors) can practice their own proofreading and editing skills. As I have noted elsewhere, "It seems to be true that it is easier to find mistakes in others' work than in one's own" (Ferris 1995c, 19). This is why newspapers, publishers, and businesses employ copy editors and proofreaders. It could be argued that students can also profitably obtain editing practice through exercises using sample student essays (i.e., not written by anyone in their class), and indeed, such activities are critical to the process of building editing-strategy skills. However, it is more engaging and motivating to work on a peer's paper currently under construction than to always look only at models, especially because the author is usually working on the same general assignment that the editor is. Thus, in conjunction with minilessons and strategy training, I like to utilize a three-stage process in which students analyze model texts, then do peer-editing activities, and then do focused self-editing (see fig. 19).

Problems with peer editing—the related issues of students not knowing what to look for and/or giving incorrect or misleading feedback—can be minimized through careful structuring and supervision of peer-editing workshops. Most teachers find it ineffective to say "Exchange papers with a partner and correct any errors you find." This task is simply too open-ended, and inevitably it leads to some students marking things wrong that are not incorrect and missing problems that really are there. Then when the authors get their papers back, they are bewildered and frustrated with feedback that they do not understand or with which they disagree. To avoid such problems, students should be **trained** in peer-editing techniques, the workshops should be carefully **structured**, and the activities should be closely **supervised** by the teachers.

As already noted, it is most effective to use peer editing as the second step of a three-stage process. Even prior to the first stage, the teacher may wish to discuss the value of such exercises with the students. This may be necessary to combat students' feelings of anxiety about trusting peers to provide good feedback and/or about their own ability to self-edit their writing. Many students feel that only the teacher, not their peers and certainly not they themselves, can provide helpful editing feedback. To make the task feel more manageable, students should first look at a sample student text and try to identify errors related to particular structures. This exercise can be done either individually or in pairs or small groups and should be debriefed with a whole-class discussion (perhaps with the text and highlighted errors up on an overhead). The instructor should help students not only to identify errors and to suggest corrections but especially to articulate explanations as to why a specific structure is correct or incorrect. In the second stage, as students move to the actual peer-editing exercise, teachers can give them handouts or instructions on the board or an overhead that ask students to look only for specific types of errors in their partner's paper, ignoring any other problems they notice (or think they see). In Exercise 2 in figure 19, for instance, peers are asked to examine their partner's use of verb tenses (both correct and incorrect) and to complete a chart with their analysis. They are specifically instructed, however, *not* to make any suggested corrections. In the follow-up self-editing stage (Exercise 3 in fig. 19), students use the information from their partner's chart to attempt corrections that appear to be necessary. During these in-class workshops, students should be encouraged to discuss any questions or disagreements, to articulate reasons or rules about why a structure is correct or incorrect, and to discuss possible alternatives to make the text more effective. They should also be allowed to ask the teacher for help in resolving questions or disagreements. The instructor may want to note questions that arise during peer-editing sessions that may be of general interest for an on-the-spot or future whole-class minilesson. If the teacher is actively engaged in monitoring peer-editing workshops, it can give him or her valuable information about the students' thought processes and about any aspects of language with which they are struggling.

Finally, the teacher should highlight the importance and value of peer- and self-editing activities by holding students accountable for doing a good job of completing them and of considering information from their partners. This can be done by asking students to submit peer-editing worksheets with final versions of their papers so that the teacher can assess both how helpful the peer editor was and whether the author grappled with the feedback he or she received. In addition, at the end of the workshop, students can be asked to write a one- or two-paragraph response to the editing activity in which they reflect on aspects of the workshop they found helpful, frustrating, or confusing and on ways in which the feedback they received will impact their writing in the future (or at least on the next draft of the paper under consideration).

Again, neither teachers nor students should mislead themselves that peer- and self-editing activities will enable student writers to find and solve all of their writing problems. However, this is not really the point of such exercises—rather, they are an integral part of an overall plan by the teacher to raise students' awareness of particularly problematic structures and to build their editing strategy skills. As long as instructors (and their students) have realistic expectations, structure and monitor activities carefully, and use them consistently and in conjunction with other parts of error treatment (teacher feedback and minilessons), they can be extremely valuable. Perhaps most importantly, they can demystify the editing process and build students' confidence that they can cope with errors and their understanding that improving written accuracy is a process that requires patience, effort, and time.

Summary

The purpose of this chapter and of this entire volume is to highlight ways in which L2 writing teachers can develop a comprehensive "error-treatment plan" for addressing issues of linguistic accuracy in student writing. Studies of error correction in writing often highlight only teacher feedback as a means to help students improve the clarity of their writing. While error feedback can be a critical component of error treatment (see chap. 4), it is not the only weapon in teachers' arsenals. When teacher feedback is combined with strategy training, grammar minilessons, and peer- and self-editing workshops, it can provide a comprehensive approach that addresses different needs and individual learning styles and that leads students toward the ultimate goal of independent self-editing.

Looking at all of these components in isolation can be a bit overwhelming for writing teachers, who wonder how they can

Phase 1: Teacher analysis of class and individual student needs, based upon student writing samples and objective tests or questionnaires
▼
Phase 2: Development of minilessons and selection of other materials for individualized work
▼
Phase 3: "Consciousness-raising" discussions and strategy-training activities
▼
Phase 4: Minilessons followed by peer- and self-editing workshops related to student essay drafts
▼
Phase 5: Teacher gives feedback on selected categories of error on student drafts, followed by in-class self-editing exercises
▼
Phase 6: Students track their progress on error logs
▼
Phase 7: Teacher examines final drafts of student writing projects to assess their progress in editing and overall accuracy
▼
The process (phases 4–7) is repeated for subsequent writing projects, with different error types being highlighted according to student need

Fig. 24. The error-treatment system: putting it all together

possibly afford the class time to incorporate all of these error-treatment components. The solution to this is to build editing as a regular, cyclical part of the writing process in the classroom. Figure 24 shows a process chart that demonstrates how all of the elements of error treatment can fit together. Figure 25 provides a suggested schedule tied to a hypothetical 15-week academic semester.

Preparing oneself to treat student error (chap. 3) and carrying out a comprehensive error-treatment plan (chaps. 4–5) can be challenging and demanding for L2 writing instructors. While no one would argue that all of teachers' time and attention should be consumed with dealing with student errors, this concern is definitely one that teachers must indeed take seriously. In many contexts, students' success or failure in their academic endeavors or their future careers may hinge in large part on their ability to improve the accuracy and clar-

Week 1: Students write diagnostic essay and complete grammar-knowledge questionnaire and pretest.

Week 3: In-class discussion about the importance of editing and introduction of general editing strategies

Week 4: Minilesson 1 (on topic selected from teacher analysis of week-1 materials); peer- and self-editing workshop on student essay drafts. Student papers then submitted to the teacher for additional feedback.

Week 5: Students receive marked papers back from teacher and complete error log. They self-edit as many errors as possible during a 20-minute in-class session (asking teacher or peers questions as needed or desired). They finalize their paper out of class and submit it for teacher feedback. The teacher's final feedback deals both with: (a) how the accuracy of the paper measures up to course grading criteria; and (b) how well students utilized self-editing techniques.

The process is repeated for successive writing cycles on a two-week schedule (see weeks 4–5).

Fig. 25. Fitting the error-treatment process into the writing-class syllabus. *Note:* The suggested schedule was designed for a university writing class meeting twice per week for 75 minutes. Many other activities—discussion of readings, instruction on and practice of writing-process strategies—are included, and error-treatment activities are integrated seamlessly with other classroom instruction.

ity of their written work. With few exceptions, it is unlikely that they will be able to achieve the high levels of accuracy demanded and expected without teacher intervention and training. While it may be tempting to simply ignore the need for error treatment, for most L2 writing teachers to do so would be to ill serve our students.

Appendixes

Appendix to Chapter 3: Sample Application Assignments for Teacher Preparation Courses

A. Assignment for Practicum Course

Have students write an in-class essay during the first week of instruction. For each student text, prepare an individualized error analysis, following the procedures and examples shown in appendix 4C and figure 9.

B. Assignments for "Teaching ESL Writing" Course

1. *In-Class Activity*

Give students three copies of an excerpt (of about 100 to 150 words, or one or two good-sized paragraphs) of an ESL student text containing a variety of error types. Tell the students to mark the text in three different ways:

- underline, circle, or highlight all errors they find;
- label errors using codes from a standard list;
- provide correct forms for all errors found.

Then discuss with students the strengths, weaknesses, and challenges they discovered with each technique. (Adapted from Ferris and Hedgcock 1998, Application Activity 5.3, 149.)

2. *Out-of-Class Assignments*

- Design and administer a survey of ESL writing teachers and/or students about their preferences as to grammar instruction and error feedback.
- Design and administer a grammar-knowledge pretest that assesses the formal knowledge of a target student population.
- Consult three or four different grammar texts to prepare a lesson on a specific grammar point.
- Design two in-class activities for grammar/editing instruction, using a sample student text for text-analysis and/or editing practice.

(Adapted from Ferris and Hedgcock 1998, Application Activities 7.1, 7.4, 7.5, and 7.6, 220–23.)

3. *Sample Questions for MA Comprehensive Examination*

You have received copies of two student papers taken from an ESL 5 class at Sacramento City College. (ESL 5 is a freshman composition course. While the course is technically equivalent to English 1A/2B at CSUS, students in this class exhibit a fairly wide range of second language and writing abilities.)

Assume that you have a diverse class of about 25 students and that it is fairly early in the semester. The papers you have are from the first out-of-class assignment the students have completed. Complete the following steps.

(a) Complete an **error analysis** for each paper, using the procedures and forms attached.

(b) Assume that the errors you found in the papers are generalizable to a significant number of students in the class. Based on your analysis, create **two 50-minute lesson plans** in which you address one or more of the problems you saw in the student papers. You may create two separate lessons on two different error/editing topics or one lesson with two connected parts. **You must use all or part of the student papers you have analyzed for at least part of your lessons.** Use the lesson-planning outline attached as a model for what to include in your lesson plans.

(c) Write a **rationale** in which you explain the results of your error analyses and how they helped you focus your lesson plans. Also explain the pedagogical choices you made in designing the lesson plans.

Appendix A to Chapter 4: Explanation of Error Types

1. **Word choice:** includes errors in which the meaning of one word is wrong or unclear in this context. Also includes wrong verb or auxiliary, modal, preposition, or relative pronoun. Does not include spelling errors, other pronoun errors, article/determiner errors.

   Examples:

   (a) *In addition* **of** *the challenge . . .* [**Possible correction:** *to*]
   (b) *My English doesn't have a very good* **prove.** [**Possible correction:** *improvement*(?)]
   (c) *I couldn't speak English as fluently as they* **were.** [**Possible correction:** *did*]

2. **Verb tense:** includes missing or erroneous verb tense markers. Also includes modals when they clearly mark tense (*would/will; can/could*). Does not include mood (subjunctive/conditional) or voice (passive/active).

   Examples:

   (a) *I* **attend** *my first year of high school.* [**Possible correction:** *attended*]
   (b) *Even though I* **have faced** *many struggles, I did not give up.* [**Possible correction:** *faced*]

3. **Verb form:** includes a wide range of errors in formation of the verb phrase not specific to time or tense markings (e.g., ill-formed passives, conditionals, and subjunctives; misuse of modals, infinitives, gerunds)

   Examples:

   (a) *They hope* **can find** *happiness.* [**Possible correction:** *to find*]
   (b) *We should let her* **knows** *it.* [**Possible correction:** *know*]

All categories and most examples are from Ferris et al. 2000 research corpus. See also table 1 and figure 12.

15. **Idioms:** includes errors in the use of idiomatic expressions

    Examples:

    (a) *People* **look down to** *others.* **[Possible correction:** *look down on*]
    (b) *I worked* **on daytime. [Possible correction:** *in the daytime*]

16. **Miscellaneous:** includes any errors that did not fit into any of the previous categories or that could not be classified

Appendix B to Chapter 4: Sample Grammar Diagnostic Materials

Note: **The following materials represent samples of grammar diagnostic materials that have been used at my institution to assess students' editing skills and familiarity with specific grammatical terms that would be covered in grammar tutorials or writing classes. They are presented for illustrative purposes only; readers should create or adapt their own diagnostic materials.**

GRAMMAR KNOWLEDGE QUESTIONNAIRE

1. In English classes you have taken before, have you ever learned any English grammar rules or terms (noun, verb, preposition, etc.)? Circle one answer.

   a. Yes, a lot   b. Sometimes   c. Very little, or never   d. Not sure

2. Has **an English teacher** ever told you that you have problems with any grammar rules? Please circle any specific problems that a teacher has told you about.

None	Nouns—plural endings	Articles
Verb tenses	Verb forms	Subject-verb agreement
Word choice	Sentence structure	

3. **In your own opinion,** what problems do you have with using English grammar in your writing? Circle all problems that you think you have.

None	Nouns—plural endings	Articles
Verb tenses	Verb forms	Subject-verb agreement
Word choice	Sentence structure	Don't know

4. Please circle ONE statement that BEST describes how you feel about your English grammar.

   a. My English grammar problems are very serious and really hurt my writing.
   b. Although I don't know much about English grammar, it's not a serious problem for me.

From Ferris and Roberts 2001, 181–82.

c. English grammar is not really a serious issue for me. Other writing issues are more important.
d. I'm not really sure whether English grammar is a problem for my writing.

5. **In your opinion,** what is the best way for me to give you feedback about grammar errors in your writing? Please circle ONE statement only.

a. Don't correct my grammar. Let me try to correct my errors myself.
b. Only correct the most serious errors.
c. Circle my errors, but don't correct them for me.
d. Circle my errors and tell me what **types of errors** they are (verb tense, word choice, etc.).
e. Correct **all** of my errors for me.

GRAMMAR KNOWLEDGE PRETEST

A. Each of the sentences below has an error in it. Using the terms from the key below, match the error type with each sentence. (Each sentence has only one error, and you will not use any error type more than once.)

ERROR TYPE KEY
a. Noun ending (plural or possessive) missing or wrong
b. Article or determiner missing or wrong
c. Verb tense wrong
d. Verb form wrong
e. Wrong word
f. Sentence structure error

1. _____ I didn't buy the car because I didn't wanted to spend so much money.

2. _____ We all rushed to help because my uncles house was on fire.

3. _____ I didn't worry about my English. Now, I understood how important it is.

4. _____ I looked at all of the cars and picked up the one I wanted.

5. _____ For immigrants there always something that makes them live unhappily in this country.

6. _____ When you are student, you always have to study hard.

B. In the student essay excerpt below, there are six errors marked. Using the same key that you used for part A above, identify each error type and suggest a correction. (Each sentence has only one error, and you will not use any error type more than once.)

College Pressures

I need to disagree with Zinsser when he states, "professors who actually like to spend time with students don't have much time to spend." I **noticed** that most professors try to spend as much time
  1
as possible with their students. I have seen many **professor** who
  2
sometimes are willing to stay half an hour after the class is over to explain to students any misunderstanding they might have **on** the
  3
material the professor is teaching.

When I think of peer pressure I see it more as an encouragement for me to succeed in a class. But Zinsser states peer pressure is a

disadvantage to a student. I disagree with him completely. When
one of my peers receives a higher grade than I do most of the time
it does not make me feel jealous or feel **pressure, instead** it makes
me understand that if I try just a little harder that I could do just as
well as the other students. **Most of friends** who I have classes with
never **have rub** in my face that they did better than me.

Appendix C to Chapter 4: Sample Error-Analysis Materials

The following materials explain how to complete an individual student error analysis and provide examples of summary forms that can be used for the analysis and/or given to the student. The same forms can be adapted to summarize data from an entire class (see fig. 9).

STUDENT PAPER ANALYSIS

To prepare the analysis, complete the following steps.

a. With a highlighter, mark errors **in the following categories:**

   subject-verb agreement
   noun ending (plural or possessive)
   determiner/article error (missing, unnecessary, wrong)
   verb tense
   verb form
   sentence fragment
   run-on sentence
   comma splice

   (You may find other error types; do not mark them. See Student Summary Report Form.)

b. Number the highlighted errors consecutively throughout the paper. Use these numbers to complete the attached Error-Analysis Sheet. For each error you will indicate its type and suggest a correction.

c. Decide on each student's most prevalent patterns of error and complete the Student Summary Report Form.

These materials were developed with support from grants from the California State University, Sacramento, Pedagogy Enhancement Program, and from the California State University Research and Creative Activity Program. (See also Ferris, Harvey, and Nuttall 1998.)

ERROR-ANALYSIS SHEET

Error Number	Type	Possible Correction
1		
2		
3		
4		
5		
6		
7		
8		
9		
10		

STUDENT SUMMARY REPORT FORM

Student name:

Tutors' names:

Tutorial number: **Day/time:**

To the student: I have carefully analyzed your first paper of the semester. I was looking to see if you had grammar mistakes from the lessons we will cover in the tutorials. The project supervisor will also be examining your final paper (at the end of the semester) to see how much progress you have made.

Error Type	Number of Errors	Error Ratio*	Ranking (most to fewest)**
Subject-verb agreement			
Noun ending (plural or possessive)			
Determiner/article error			
Verb tense			
Verb form			
Sentence fragment			
Run-on sentence			
Comma splice			

*The **error ratio** was calculated by dividing the number of errors in each category by the total errors found. The larger the ratio, the more serious the error.

1 = most and 8 = fewest. If you had **no errors in a particular category, it was marked **N/A (not applicable).**

Other errors: **I also found examples of the following error types, which are NOT covered in the tutorial curriculum.**

Appendix D to Chapter 4: Marked Student Papers with Analyses

Note: **Here are two sets of papers written by two different university ESL writers and marked by two different teachers. Each set includes a preliminary draft with the teacher's error markings reproduced, an analysis of the teacher's markings, the student's revised draft, and an analysis of each student's progress. A comparison of students/teachers is provided at the end of the appendix.**

Student 1—Draft A

Conflicts of Cultural and Languages Metamorphosis

Minorities are groups of people that have in common ethnic, racial, or religion, [WF WF] especially when it constitute a small quantity of a population. [PR] Minorities often have fewer rights and less power than majority groups. One reason of the existence of minorities is immigration. When culture and class difference between groups of people, it can cause inequalities or discrimination. Being a minority group affect a person identity in a negative way, specially when you are different in culture and race.

I grow up being a minority group in my native country Panama. [VT] "This affects a person's identity radically". I can say that for my experience. Just for being the minority group, most of the time you are the target of their criticism. [I am] If you get something well done they get jealous, in contrast they laugh. When you are the minority [people?] group you feel like in another world even though you are in the same country. You want to be accepted by them. You don't want to be a lonely wolf, you want to be in the pack of wolves.

I have to deal my Spanish at school and Chinese at home. [w/] It is hard to go on with this two different languages and culture. [N] Usually when I'm outside or in my native country the people can't image that I'm Panamanian they judge the physical appearance. [RO] That gave me a lot of hard time, since child: Is the color of the skin so important? [VT (use present perfect)] [WF]

"Who I am?", A Chinese or Panamanian? I have to find out some answers to so many

Papers are from the Ferris et al. 2000 research corpus and are used with student/teacher permission.

questions. I think that I'm both of them, Chinese and Panamanian. But if I have to choose only one, I think is Chinese. [VF] (Because I have absorb [FRAG] the most part of the Chinese culture than Panamanian culture.) Being the minority isn't bad because you always could get positive consequences from any kind of situation. I have the opportunity to experience more than one culture, [RO] however being grown up [growing up?] in the minority group feel [VT?] confusing because your long-awaited feelings doesn't develop that suddenly.

In "A Story of Conflicts" Yeshia [SP] Aslanian [SV] describe about his internal conflict that happen [VT] when he was a child and when he came into the United States, [RO] he has [VT] to struggle with the two languages and cultures, as I do. I have the Panamanian accent but just by looking different it also affect [SV] me a little bit, because not only culture makes me a minority, [but] Also my race is different from them. I often heard [VT] them saying something about me of being [people], but I'm Panamanian too. They don't realize that I born [VF] there too. The way people look at you [PR] is somehow different. They only judge the external appearance, they just look the difference between and you [PR] and them. It is like comparing a diamond to a diamond ring, a diamond is still a diamond with or without the ring. But somehow people really cares if you wear a ring like them or not...

Therefore, a minority group has to face many obstacle [N] and after them, the reward [N] are satisfactory, like being bilingual, etc. However, a minority group is an easy target of the inequalities and discrimination of people.

Analysis of teacher marking: This teacher was a voluntary participant in the Ferris et al. 2000 study, meaning that she had agreed to mark all student papers comprehensively, using the error-correction log outlined in figure 12 and described in appendix 4A. However, careful examination of this student paper shows that her marking was far from comprehensive. A number of language errors fitting the categories in figure 12 were left unmarked. For instance, in the first three sentences of the third paragraph, there are several verb tense errors that the teacher did not mark, though she did note such errors elsewhere. When she did use error codes, she appeared to stick closely with the codes provided (fig .12). In addition, she added some direct corrections, particularly crossing out unnecessary words, inserting missing words or suffixes, and suggesting rewordings in a couple of spots.

Student 1—Draft B (revised)

Conflicts of Cultural and Languages Metamorphosis

Minorities are groups of people that have in common ethnicity, race, or religion, especially when they constitute a small quantity of a population. Minorities often have fewer rights and less power than majority groups. One reason of the existence of minorities is immigration. When culture and class difference between groups of people, it can cause inequalities or discrimination. Being a minority group affects a person's identity in a negative way, specially when you are different in culture and race.

I grow up being a minority in my native country Panama. This affects a person's identity radically. I can say that for my experience. Just for being the minority group, most of the time I am the target of their criticism. If I get something well done they get jealous, otherwise they laugh. When people are the minority group they feel like in another world even though they are in the same country. I want to be accepted by them. I don't want to be a lonely wolf, I want to be in the pack of wolves.

I have to deal my Spanish at school and Chinese at home. It is hard to go on with these two different languages and cultures. Usually when I'm outside or in my native country the people can't image that I'm Panamanian. They judge the physical appearance. That gave me a lot of hard time, since I was a child: Is the color of the skin so important? "Who I am?", A Chinese or Panamanian? I have to find out some answers to so many questions. I think that I'm both of them, Chinese and Panamanian. But if I have to choose only one, I think it is Chinese, because I have absorbed the most part of the Chinese culture than Panamanian culture.

It is true that everyone always could get positive consequences from any kind of circumstances, including being a minority. I have the opportunity to experience more than one culture, however growing up in the minority group feels confusing, because my long-awaited feelings don't develop that suddenly. It doesn't takes days to a person to realize who they are. It takes several months or even years to define who we are, especially being a minority.

In "A Story of Conflicts" Yeghia Aslanian describes about his internal conflict that happened when he was a child and when he came into the United States. He had to struggle with the two languages and cultures, as I do. I have the Panamanian accent but just by looking different it also affects me a little bit, because not only culture makes me a minority, but also my race is different from them. I often hear them saying something about me of Chinese people, but I'm Panamanian too. They don't realize that I was born there too. The way people look at me is somehow different. They only judge the external appearance; they just look at the difference between me and them. It is like comparing a diamond to a diamond ring, a diamond is still a diamond with or without the ring. But somehow people really care if you wear a ring like them or not…

Therefore, a minority group has to face many obstacle and after them, the reward are satisfactory, like being bilingual, etc. However, a minority group is an easy target of the inequalities and discrimination of people.

Analysis: The student successfully incorporated nearly all of the corrections, whether direct or indirect, indicated by the teacher on the previous draft. However, errors left unmarked by the teacher were not addressed by the student in the revision.

Student 2—Draft A

Identity is the qualities someone has that make him/her different from other people. A persons identity plays a bigger role in their life. No matter where we go, either going to church, school, or moving to another country, our identity reveals who we are. It shows that cultural, custom and language identify our identity. This identity is challenged when we come as a minority to a new culture.

One of the challenges is trying to assimilate into the new culture. My own experience reveals these problems of assimilation. When I was in high school, I felt that the world was laying on my shoulders, just thinking of making new friends with the Americans. I had all sorts of questions that popped into my head, "Are they going to accept me because I have a brown skin, has an accent, and a black hair." Also being able for me to have the perfect English to communicate, challenged me a lot. It motivated me to try harder. Since English is spoken language here, I needed to learn it. However, I felt that much like the author of "A Story of Conflicts". In this article, Yeghia Aslanian says, "I began to devote my self to Persian—reading, copying, and memorizing long stretches of Persian texts". Therefore, I have hope that it would lead me to success. Even today, I do feel that I do not belong here since I could not communicate very well. I feel that part of my identity has been stripped from me. and it was one of the sacrifice that I made when I moved here. However, it did not stop me from trying to learn to write and speak in English.

Another challenge facing a minority is coming into contact with an entirely new culture with different values. The culture in here is totally different than the one that I~~,~~[was] accustomed to in the Philippines. ~~As~~ I observe[that] some teenagers here they do not have much respect for their parents and elders. In ~~addition~~[fact], they usually talk back to ~~their~~[them] ~~parents.~~ I just could not imagine doing that to my parents. At the same time, [the] Philippines is a conservative country while the U.S. is ~~a~~ modern country. However, I am in a different country and I have to open my eyes with all the new things that I am surrounded with like new culture, customs, and religion.

In addition~~of~~[to] the challenge that a minority has to face is how much freedom they have in religion and speech ~~in~~ here. It shocked me. In the Philippines, we do not get that much freedom with these. ~~All I know is that~~ we just have to follow the rules and be numb to voice out [?] what we think is right to the government or else you will pay the consequences. Also, ~~how diverse~~[is so diverse] the U.S. ~~with~~ religion while [in] the Philippines, they only see one religion, the Roman Catholic.

When we move to another country, we do not think that [it] will become a minority. Therefore, our identity shows ~~of~~ who we are and we have to accept the challenges that we face as a minority, like learning the language and new culture.

Analysis of teacher marking: This instructor clearly abandoned the error-correction system agreed upon for the research project, ignoring the error codes and providing only direct correction. Again, his corrections were not comprehensive, as several problematic constructions are left unmarked (see the third sentence in paragraph two, for example). More striking is his arguably appropriative use of correction to change constructions that were not grammatically wrong to suit his own style preferences. Examples of this include the following.

Student's sentence: In ***addition,*** they usually talk back to ***their parents.***
Teacher's correction: In ***fact,*** they usually talk back to ***them.***

Even worse, the teacher at points provides direct corrections that actually lead the student to make an error.

Student's sentence: When we move to another country, we do not think that will become a minority.

Teacher's correction: . . . we do not think that *it* will become a minority.

Student 2—Draft B (revised)

Identity is the qualities someone has that make him/her different from other people. A persons identity plays a bigger role in their life. No matter where we go, either to church, school, or to another country, our identity reveals who we are. It shows our culture, custom and language to others. However, this identity is challenged when we come as a minority to a new culture.

One of these challenges is trying to assimilate into the new culture. My own experience reveals these problems of assimilation. When I was in high school, I felt that the world was laying on my shoulders, just thinking of making new friends with the Americans. I had all sorts of questions that popped into my head, "Are they going to accept me because I have a brown skin, an accent, and black hair." Also being able to communicate in English challenged me a lot. It motivated me to try harder. Since English is spoken here, I needed to learn it. However, I felt that much like the author of "A Story of Conflicts." In this article, Yeghia Aslanian says, "I began to devote my self to Persian—reading, copying, and memorizing long stretches of Persian texts." I, too, have hope that it would lead me to success. Even today, I feel that I do not belong here since I can not communicate very well. I feel that part of my identity has been stripped from me. It was one of the sacrifice that I made when I moved here. However, it did not stop me from trying to learn to write and speak in English.

Another challenge facing a minority is coming into contact with an entirely new culture with different values. The culture in here is totally different than the one that I was accustomed to in the Philippines. I observe some teenagers here do not have much respect for their parents and elders. In fact, they usually talk back to them. I just could not imagine doing that to my parents. Eventhough, the Philippines has a very different way of raising children, I realize now in a new country. Thus, I have to open my eyes to all the new things that I am surrounded with, like new culture, customs, and religion.

In addition to the challenge that a minority has to face is how much freedom they have in religion and speech here. It shocked me. In the Philippines, we do not get that much freedom with these. We just have to follow the rules and be numb to say what we think is right to the government or else you will pay the consequences. Also the U.S. is so diverse in religion while the Philippines, they only see one religion, the Roman Catholic.

When we move to another country, we do not think that it will become a minority. Our culture, customs, and language will be challenge when we are in a different country. Therefore, our identity shows who we are and we have to accept the challenges that we face as a minority, like learning the language and new culture.

Analysis: This student transferred virtually all of the teacher's direct corrections into his revision and did not correct errors left unmarked.

Comparison: Though the two teachers had radically different approaches to marking errors, the revision outcomes were similar: The two student writers made changes, mostly successfully, to nearly all of the items marked in the preliminary drafts. However, where errors were left unmarked, neither student independently initiated corrections.

One conclusion that could be drawn is that it matters little whether teachers use direct or indirect correction, since the revision outcomes appear to be the same. On the other hand, student 1 was forced to think about the error codes and provide the correct forms while student 2 merely had to copy what the teacher had provided. Other things being equal, it seems clear that student 1 is likely to learn and retain more from this correction-revision cycle than student 2. In fact, an independent longitudinal analysis completed by Ferris and Helt (2000) showed that the classmates of student 1 made substantially more progress in error reduction over the course of a semester than those of student 2. Further, the possible demotivating (or even confusing or frustrating) effects of the second teacher's appropriative correction behaviors should be considered.

Appendix A to Chapter 5: Ideas for Surveying Faculty or Local Employers about the Importance of Errors in L2 Student Writing

Option 1: Student writing sample

Prepare a one-page handout that includes a student essay excerpt (one or two paragraphs long) that contains errors representative in type and frequency of students in your class. Ask a sample of either faculty (both English/ESL and subject-matter) or local employers to read the student sample and respond to the following questions.

- Is the ability to write clearly in English important for success in your class (workplace)? Why or why not?
- If the above essay excerpt is representative of that student's ability to communicate in English, do you think this individual would be able to pass your class (succeed in your workplace)? Please comment on why or why not.
- If a nonnative speaker of English with writing skills equivalent to those of the student who wrote this sample was in your class (or was a prospective employee), what would be your reaction? What advice or assistance might you give that individual to help them succeed?

Option 2: Survey or interview questions

Find a sample of "informants" (English/ESL instructors, subject-matter faculty in disciplines that your ESL students might pursue, or prospective employers) and ask them to respond to the following questions (either in writing, via E-mail, or in interviews in person or over the phone).

1. Is the ability to write clearly in English important for success in your class (workplace)? Why or why not?
2. Have you had ESL students (employees) in your class (workplace) before? Was their ability to write clearly and grammatically ever a problem for them or for you? Please explain.
3. If you have had ESL students (employees) with writing problems before, what types of language problems did they have? (Please be as specific as you can.)

4. Would you consider hiring (or allowing into your class) nonnative speakers of English who made frequent or systematic errors in grammar, spelling, punctuation, or vocabulary? Why or why not?
5. If you would hire them (or allow them to take your class), would it be important for you that they attempt to improve the accuracy and clarity of their writing? How might you help them or motivate them to improve?

Appendix B to Chapter 5: Student Consciousness-Raising Exercise with Sample Student Paper

Instructions: The student paper below was written for a previous class during the first week of the semester. Errors in grammar, vocabulary, spelling, and punctuation are in bold, and a summary of errors appears on the next page.

Read the student paper and look at the course-grading criteria (especially the criteria for a "4" [passing] paper and a "3" [failing] paper) (see fig. 16). Discuss the following questions with your instructor and classmates.

- **Considering *errors only*, if this paper were written for the final, do you think the student would pass the class? Why or why not?**
- **What are the most frequent *types* of errors you see in this essay?**

Student Paper

Opertunity is a very important **alternative** that everyone should take. Taking on the **opertunity** will only benefit you in skills and in more **advantage** ways. The **opertunity** to encourage others will soon come back to you **as** in the same way. **Opertunity** will only **past you one time around** to see if you'll take the chance.

Once in a life time an **opertunity** will appear to those who have hope in another person. Giving others the courage to succeed will benefit them and soon **the courage will come to you.** The **opertunity** to make someone feel right **inside of them** is the **opertunity** for you to take **pride you've** done something good for your self. I remember a time when I treated everyone with **the** respect and they really **appreciate** what **I've** given them. Now, they're treating me the same way as before **w/ the** respect and caring.

Skills is one of the most important thing in life and in order to have some skills you'll have to **take on experimenting the opertunity** that comes your way. **Opertunity maybe** hard or easy at some point, but it's knowledge that you need to **take to your brain.** However, **opertunity** is like having **more advantage at** those who do not have the **opertunity.** For example I'm applying for Apple Computer Inc. and one of **my is** also applying, but I had the **opertunity to go through high school taking some course of computer** and my friend **don't. it** will more **likly** be that **I'm getting** hired and he **don't,** just because I had the **opertunity** to take **some course** in high school and **he don't** so **I'm at a more advantage.**

Source: Ferris & Roberts 2000 research corpus. Used with permission.

Analysis

Verb errors	9
Noun ending errors	2
Article errors	3
Word choice errors	3
Sentence structure errors	8
Total errors marked	**25**
Total words	**279**

Appendix C to Chapter 5: Error-Analysis Procedures and Student Summary Form

Procedures

1. With a highlighter, look carefully through the essay. Highlight and consecutively number every error you find.

2. Use the attached Error-Analysis Sheet to categorize and offer a correction for each error.

3. Use the Error-Analysis Summary Form to total up the types of errors and numbers of each error. Then identify the three most significant problems and write them in on the bottom of the form. *Note:* The "most serious problem" is not always the most *frequent* problem.

4. Return all of the above materials to the student writers, keeping a copy of the summary form for your own future reference.

ERROR-ANALYSIS SHEET

Error Number	Type	Possible Correction
1		
2		
3		
4		
5		
6		
7		
8		
9		
10		
11		
12		
13		
14		
15		
16		
17		
18		

ERROR-ANALYSIS SUMMARY FORM—DIAGNOSTIC ESSAY

Student name: _____

Error Type	Total Number of Errors and Ratio of Total
Verb tense or form	
Noun endings	
Articles/determiners	
Word choice or form	
Sentence structure: missing or unnecessary words, word order	
Sentence structure: fragments, run-ons, comma splices	
Spelling	
Mechanics: punctuation or capitalization	
Other_____	
Other_____	

Most serious errors to work on:

1.
2.
3.

Appendix D to Chapter 5: Minilesson on Understanding Shifts from Present to Past Tense

1. Time Signals in Writing

Tenses occur in clusters (groups) according to the time frame (now, before now) of the text. A switch from the present-future cluster to the past cluster or from the past cluster to the present-future cluster often goes along with a **time signal** (*now, yesterday, last week, last year, soon*) that helps the reader to understand that you are switching tenses.

Look at the example paragraph below and notice how the verb tenses change after the time markers (*last year; Now that I am home*).

I **don't like** traveling. I **think** traveling **is** expensive, tiring, and stressful, and expensive. But *last year,* before I **went** to London, I **thought** traveling to another country **would** be exciting and glamorous. *Now that I am home* from my trip, I **feel** differently.

2. Exercise: Examining Verb Tenses

Examine the 14 highlighted verb phrases in the paragraphs (from an essay entitled "Robo Teacher") that follow. Above each, say whether it refers to past time or to present-future time. When there is a switch from one cluster to another, try to explain the reasons for the switch. Also underline any time markers you find. *Note:* Do not worry about separating the verbs into separate tenses such as "present perfect" or "past progressive." For now, just divide them into "past" versus "present-future" time.

I once **heard** my aunt, herself a teacher, speculate on why educators **refuse** to use computers to their full capacity. She **said** many teachers **are** afraid that they would be eventually replaced by teaching machines.

This idea **interested** me, so over the years **I have watched** teachers to decide whether or not they could be replaced by robots. My conclusion is that the best teachers could never possibly be replaced by machines, but to save money, the mediocre ones could be—in fact, should be—replaced.

It's easy to describe the replaceable teacher. This **is** the teacher whose most challenging task **is** to repeat everything in the textbook in front of the class. This teacher **begins** class by checking his lesson plan to see what page the class **is** on in The Book. He then **orders** us to take out our homework (questions from The

Book **answered** in complete sentences) and to raise our hands if we **have had** problems answering any of the questions.

3. Exercise: Examining Your Own Writing

Look at the essay you wrote at the beginning of this chapter (or any other recent piece of writing you have done). Highlight all of the verb phrases and mark which ones are in the "present-future" or "past" cluster, as you did in Exercise 2 above. Also mark any time markers you find, especially those that signal a tense shift. *Note:* Not all verb phrases will have tense markers. Just mark the ones you are sure are either "present-future" or "past."

4. Exercise: Identifying Errors in Verb Tense

Some of the sentences below contain errors in verb tense. If the tense of the highlighted verb is correct, write "C." If it is incorrect, write "I," try to explain why it is wrong, and suggest a correct form.

___ 1. When I was shopping with my mother, I soon **discover** that people could tell that I was not one of them.
___ 2. Sundara's aunt didn't want to her to date an American, but **wants** her to see a Khmer boy.
___ 3. American culture **is** a mixture of many other cultures.
___ 4. The clerk **is** rude when he spoke to my dad in a loud voice.
___ 5. I told my dad I **know** where the nuts and bolts are.
___ 6. As my father and I **walked** away from the counter, I started to hear the employees laughing at us.
___ 7. As each day **goes** by, I was becoming more exposed to the other cultures in America.
___ 8. I believe that it is not possible for immigrants to be truly happy in America if they **did** nothing to help themselves.
___ 9. After he and his family came to America, he **dropped** out of school to help support his family for a while.
___ 10. I **grow** up being a minority in my native country, Panama.

(Source of examples: Ferris et al. 2000 research corpus. Used with permission.)

5. Exercise: Verb Tense Editing

Read through the student essay and highlight or underline every verb or verb phrase. Some of the verbs have errors in tense. Circle the verbs you think have tense errors. Be prepared to explain to a partner why you think those verbs are incorrect while the others are correct.

Children start learning how to write more from their parents than any other people. Therefore, parents are big influences on their kids. Children need their parents' encouragement. They also need a good environment to study in.

When I was a child, my parents spent their spare time helping me read newspapers. My father encouraged me to read by telling me that he wanted me to read all news. My father expected me to be good in school. He never forced me to read or write, but he always said, "Spending your spare time in reading and writing will help your knowledge improve." My father wanted to take me to the library every weekend. However, we lived in a poor country with few books and no public libraries. Therefore, my father took me to a small bookstore which was far away from my home. I started reading the Saigon news. Six months later, I realized that my reading had improve. This time I read by myself, and I don't wait until my father asked me to read. I volunteered to read for my father. One day he said, "Compared to other kids who are the same age as you, you are a very good kid because you are my good son." I was very happy when he said "because you are my good son." I promise myself that I would do whatever my father expected me to do. The way my parents influence me is very simple, but it's very important for me to take his advice to improve my reading.

In my experience, having a good place to study is very important. For myself, my father had create a good environment for me even though we live in a tiny house. He make a small table for me to read and write in a corner of the house. He said, "This is your private place to study. You can read and write whatever you feel like." My father not only made the table, but he also bought me some short stories to read.

These are the ways my parents influence my reading and writing. I believe it is unnecessary to have parents who have a high level of education. It is important how parents encourage their children.

(Source of student essay: Ferris and Roberts 2001 research corpus. Used with permission.)

Appendix E to Chapter 5: Minilesson on "Untreatable" Errors in Word Choice

A. DEFINITION

1. *Word Choice errors* occur when either (a) the wrong word is used in a particular sentence; or (b) the wrong word form (e.g., an adjective instead of a noun) is used.

   Examples

   1a. I kept myself **concentrated** on my studies. [This should be **focused.**]
   1b. I had to translate **to** him. [This should be **for.**]

   2a. America is considered a melting pot, so being **multiculture** would be a positive aspect in this country. [**Culture** is a noun, but the adjective form, **cultural,** is required here.]
   2b. I can **communication** with my family by speaking Chinese. [**Communication** is a noun, but the verb form, **communicate,** is required here.]

B. SOURCES OF WORD CHOICE ERRORS

1. Choosing the wrong word form (noun instead of adjective, etc.). (See 2a and 2b.)

2. Choosing a word that has a similar meaning to the word you need but that doesn't fit grammatically into the sentence. (See 1a—**concentrate** and **focus** are similar in meaning, but while you can **focus yourself,** you cannot **concentrate yourself.**)

3. Choosing the wrong preposition. (See 1b.)

4. Choosing a word that sounds like the word you need but that has a different meaning.

   Examples

   a. Because of my **flowing** English, people do not stare at me anymore. [The writer meant **fluent.**]
   b. At a wedding, the bride and groom **change their vowels.** [This should be **exchange their vows.**]
   c. The tension was its **pick.** [This should be **peak.**]

5. Not proofreading carefully and making "careless" errors in writing or typing.

   Examples

   a. Have you done your **homeword?** [This should be **homework.**]
   b. My parents never read books to **my.** [This should be **me.**]

C. PRACTICE EXERCISE 1

Examine the sentences following (word choice errors are highlighted). See if you can determine (a) the source of the error and (b) what a possible correction might be. *Note:* There may be more than one way to correct a particular error.

1. Before I came to America **for studying** for a bachelor's degree . . .

2. As **longer** as I live here, the more problems I find.

3. I was **educated** that class time is very serious and that telling jokes to teachers is not proper at that time.

4. Minorities are people that have in common **ethnic, racial,** or religion.

5. A **parent** language is **importance** because it affects a person's identity.

6. Not only has my cultural barrier been **coming alone,** but there are also other barriers that have an **affect** on my life as well.

7. People **immigrant** to another country.

8. Living without **dependent** on parents, I can build up more confidence and learn how to take care of myself.

9. In order for minority groups to **bind** into the United States, they must **accommodate** to the new culture.

10. They will **be** more opportunity **in** study.

D. EDITING GUIDE: AVOIDING WORD CHOICE ERRORS

1. Be sure that you understand the differences between **noun, verb, adjective, and adverb** forms of different words (*beauty, beautify, beautiful, beautifully*) and which form to use in a particular sentence.
   Strategy: Determine what part of speech is appropriate for the sentence and then check a dictionary for the appropriate form.

2. For preposition errors, try checking a dictionary such as *Longman's* to see which prepositions go with particular verbs. (Look up the specific verb and see if there is any information about accompanying prepositions.) If not, you may wish to ask a native speaker for help with this—prepositions can be very troublesome.

3. If you know that you make word choice errors because of hurrying and not proofreading carefully, be sure to leave enough time to read over your paper before turning it in—this is the type of error that reading aloud may help you find.

4. Be careful when using a thesaurus (either a book or a computer version). Just

't mean they can be used in
focus myself but not con-
g the word correctly and can't
speaker to help you. Rules

ce errors—these can be very
sure you have selected the right
nds like the one you want!
ask for help. If you are still not
rd that you *are* sure about!

the various types we have
went wrong, and suggest a
ce error in some passages.

ad.

didn't go to college, so he
did. At the beginning I was
ntry I never passed by this

eak English as fluently as they

rity had many positive and

ling I could speak English to

'A" average to meet people's
school she neglected the

7. However, in America, the Chinese were treated as a minority group where I was treated exactly the opposite comparing to my native country.

8. For example, my childhood experience was not fulfilled with happiness.

Notes

Chapter 2

This critical examination of the literature was drawn from several sources: searches of computerized databases, such as *Dissertation Abstracts,* ERIC, and LLBA; printed annotated bibliographies (*Research in the Teaching of English;* Silva, Brice, and Reichelt 1999; Tannacito 1995); and unpublished master's theses and conference papers of which I have become aware. I include recent papers from this last category in an effort to provide as comprehensive an overview as possible. However, being aware of the pitfalls of including unrefereed research studies in a review, I have avoided using an unpublished source as the sole support for any particular assertion or generalization.

1. Cohen and Cavalcanti (1990) also report not only differences in error-correction patterns across the three teachers but substantial differences in the number of comments given across the ability levels of the student writers.
2. Teacher interviews further suggest that at least in some cases in which errors were left unmarked, this was due to the instructors' intentional decision to be selective in marking major patterns of error rather than to be comprehensive (marking all observed errors). See Komura 1999 for further discussion.
3. Ferris (1997) does note that in some cases these verbal comments were "paired with underlined examples of particular error patterns in the body of the essay" (327), but these were clearly intended to be illustrative of the verbal comments rather than comprehensive in-text correction of all errors.
4. In Frantzen's (1995) study, groups that received direct and indirect feedback were compared. The "direct-feedback" (experimental) group did not show progress in accuracy and in fact increased their error ratios on one grammatical construction. However, the "indirect-feedback" (control) group did make measurable progress in accuracy.
5. As already noted, Polio, Fleck, and Leder's (1998) study showed no significant differences between the error-correction and control (no-feedback) groups. However, the authors do note that both groups of students improved in accuracy over the seven-week duration of the study.

6. Semke's (1984) study also compared feedback treatment groups, again reporting no significant differences across subject groups. However, since Semke does not report pretest results, it cannot be determined whether or not progress was made across the treatment groups—only that their post-test measures showed no significant differences.
7. It has been pointed out to me (Belcher and Liu, personal communication) that there may well be some dispute as to whether all errors in article usage and verb tense/form are truly treatable, under my definition. While Belcher and Liu's point is well taken and should be investigated empirically, I believe that the distinction and categories outlined here serve for the sake of starting a discussion about how to treat different broad subtypes of written error.
8. It is also worth noting that in Ferris et al.'s (2000) longitudinal study, the error-correction success rates in revision were quite high for both treatable and untreatable error categories.
9. In fact, some researchers have expressed concern that peer-editing sessions will harm student writers more than they help because of L2 writers' relative lack of linguistic competence (see Leki 1990).
10. The studies by Komura (1999), Roberts (1999), and Ferris and Helt (2000) utilized the same database. Roberts's study was a case-study analysis of eight students, while Ferris and Helt's study was a text-analytic study of 55 ESL writers.

Chapter 3

1. To add further fuel to the fire, Messerschmitt (1998) reported that, in a survey of ESL employers in the San Francisco Bay Area, the inadequacy of MA TESOL graduates in handling grammar issues was identified as the most glaring weakness noted by prospective employers.

References

Ascher, A. 1993. *Think about editing.* Boston: Heinle and Heinle.

Ashwell, T. 2000. Patterns of teacher response to student writing in a multiple-draft composition classroom: Is content feedback followed by form feedback the best method? *Journal of Second Language Writing* 9:227–58.

Atwell, N. 1998. *In the middle: New understandings about writing, reading, and learning.* 2d ed. Portsmouth, N.H.: Boynton/Cook Heinemann.

Bates, L., J. Lane, and E. Lange. 1993. *Writing clearly: Responding to ESL compositions.* Boston: Heinle and Heinle.

Berger, V. 1990. The effects of peer and self-feedback. *CATESOL Journal* 3:21–35.

Biber, D. 1988. *Variation in speech and writing.* Cambridge: Cambridge University Press.

Biber, D., S. Johansson, G. Leech, S. Conrad, and E. Finegan. 1999. *Longman grammar of spoken and written English.* London: Longman.

Brannon, L., and C. H. Knoblauch. 1982. On students' rights to their own texts: A model of teacher response. *College Composition and Communication* 33:157–66.

Brice, C. 1995. ESL writers' reactions to teacher commentary: A case study. Paper presented at the Thirtieth Annual TESOL Convention, March 28–April 2, 1995, Long Beach, Calif. (ERIC Document Reproduction Service No. ED394 312).

Brice, C., and L. Newman. 2000. The case against grammar correction in practice: What do students think? Paper presented at the Symposium on Second Language Writing, September 15–16, 2000, Purdue University, West Lafayette, Ind.

Brown, H. D. 1994. *Principles of language learning and teaching.* 3d ed. Englewood Cliffs, N.J.: Prentice-Hall.

Burt, M. K., and C. Kiparsky. 1972. *The gooficon: A repair manual for English.* Rowley, Mass.: Newbury House.

Byrd, P. 1998. Grammar in the composition syllabus. In *Grammar in the composition classroom: Essays on teaching ESL for college-bound students,* by P. Byrd and J. Reid, 33–53. Boston: Heinle and Heinle.

Byrd, P., and J. M. Reid. 1998. *Grammar in the composition classroom: Essays on teaching ESL for college-bound students.* Boston: Heinle and Heinle.

Chandler, J. 2000. The efficacy of error correction for improvement in the accuracy of L2 student writing. Paper presented at the American Association of Applied Linguistics Conference, March, Vancouver, B.C.

Chaney, S. J. 1999. The effect of error types on error correction and revision. Master's thesis, California State University, Sacramento.

Cohen, A. 1987. Student processing of feedback on their compositions. In *Learner strategies in language learning,* ed. A. L. Wenden and J. Rubin, 57–69. Englewood Cliffs, N.J.: Prentice-Hall.

Cohen, A., and M. Cavalcanti. 1990. Feedback on written compositions: Teacher and student verbal reports. In *Second language writing: Research insights for the classroom,* ed. B. Kroll, 155–77. Cambridge: Cambridge University Press.

Cohen, A., and M. Robbins. 1976. Toward assessing interlanguage performance: The relationship between selected errors, learners' characteristics, and learners' expectations. *Language Learning* 26:45–66.

Connor, U. 1996. *Contrastive rhetoric: Cross-cultural aspects of second-language writing.* Cambridge: Cambridge University Press.

Connor, U., and A. M. Johns, eds. 1990. *Coherence in writing: Research and pedagogical perspectives.* Alexandria, Va.: TESOL.

Connor, U., and R. B. Kaplan, eds. 1987. *Writing across languages: Analysis of L2 text.* Reading, Mass.: Addison-Wesley.

Corder, S. P. 1971. Idiosyncratic dialects and error analysis. *International Review of Applied Linguistics* 9 (2): 147–60.

Doughty, C., and J. Williams, eds. 1998. *Focus on form in classroom second language acquisition.* Cambridge: Cambridge University Press.

Ellis, R. 1998. Teaching and research: Options in grammar teaching. *TESOL Quarterly* 32:39–60.

Enginarlar, H. 1993. Student response to teacher feedback in EFL writing. *System* 21:193–204.

Eskey, D. E. 1983. Meanwhile, back in the real world . . . : Accuracy and fluency in second language teaching. *TESOL Quarterly* 17:315–23.

Fathman, A., and E. Whalley. 1990. Teacher response to student writing: Focus on form versus content. In *Second language writing: Research insights for the classroom,* ed. B. Kroll, 178–90. Cambridge: Cambridge University Press.

Ferris, D. R. 1995a. Can advanced ESL students be taught to correct their most serious and frequent errors? *CATESOL Journal* 8 (1): 41–62.

———. 1995b. Student reactions to teacher response in multiple-draft composition classrooms. *TESOL Quarterly* 29:33–53.

———. 1995c. Teaching ESL composition students to become independent self-editors. *TESOL Journal* 4 (4): 18–22.

———. 1997. The influence of teacher commentary on student revision. *TESOL Quarterly* 31:315–39.

———. 1999a. The case for grammar correction in L2 writing classes: A response to Truscott (1996). *Journal of Second Language Writing* 8:1–10.

———. 1999b. One size does not fit all: Response and revision issues for immigrant student writers. In *Generation 1.5 meets college composi-*

tion, ed. L. Harklau, K. Losey, and M. Siegal, 143–57. Mahwah, N.J.: Lawrence Erlbaum Associates.

Ferris, D. R., S. J. Chaney, K. Komura, B. J. Roberts, and S. McKee. 2000. Perspectives, problems, and practices in treating written error. Colloquium presented at International TESOL Convention, March 14–18, 2000, Vancouver, B.C.

Ferris, D. R., H. Harvey, and G. Nuttall. 1998. Assessing a joint training project: Editing strategies for ESL teachers and students. Paper presented at the annual meeting of the American Association of Applied Linguistics, March, Seattle, Wash.

Ferris, D. R., and J. S. Hedgcock. 1998. *Teaching ESL composition: Purpose, process, and practice.* Mahwah, N.J.: Lawrence Erlbaum Associates.

Ferris, D. R., and M. Helt. 2000. Was Truscott right? New evidence on the effects of error correction in L2 writing classes. Paper presented at the American Association of Applied Linguistics Conference, March 11–14, 2000, Vancouver, B.C.

Ferris, D. R., S. Pezone, C. R. Tade, and S. Tinti. 1997. Teacher commentary on student writing: Descriptions and implications. *Journal of Second Language Writing* 6:155–82.

Ferris, D. R., and B. Roberts. 2001. Error feedback in L2 writing classes: How explicit does it need to be? *Journal of Second Language Writing* 10:161–84.

Fox, L. 1992. *Focus on editing.* London: Longman.

Frantzen, D. 1995. The effects of grammar supplementation on written accuracy in an intermediate Spanish content course. *Modern Language Journal* 79:329–44.

Frantzen, D., and D. Rissell. 1987. Learner self-correction of written compositions: What does it show us? In *Foreign language learning: A research perspective,* ed. B. VanPatten, T. R. Dvorak, and J. F. Lee, 92–107. Cambridge: Newbury House.

Frodesen, J. 1991. Grammar in writing. In *Teaching English as a second or foreign language,* 2d ed., ed. M. Celce-Murcia, 264–76. Boston: Heinle and Heinle.

Goldstein, L., and S. Conrad. 1990. Student input and the negotiation of meaning in ESL writing conferences. *TESOL Quarterly* 24:443–60.

Hedgcock, J., and N. Lefkowitz. 1994. Feedback on feedback: Assessing learner receptivity in second language writing. *Journal of Second Language Writing* 3:141–63.

———. 1996. Some input on input: Two analyses of student response to expert feedback on L2 writing. *Modern Language Journal* 80:287–308.

Hendrickson, J. M. 1978. Error correction in foreign language teaching: Recent theory, research, and practice. *Modern Language Journal* 62:387–98.

———. 1980. The treatment of error in written work. *Modern Language Journal* 64:216–21.

Higgs, T., and R. Clifford. 1982. The push toward communication. In *Curriculum, competence, and the foreign language teacher,* ed. T. Higgs, 57–79. Skokie, Ill.: National Textbook Co.

Horowitz, D. 1986. Process not product: Less than meets the eye. *TESOL Quarterly* 20:141–44.

James, C. 1998. *Errors in language learning and use: Exploring error analysis.* London: Longman.

Janopolous, M. 1992. University faculty tolerance of NS and NNS writing errors. *Journal of Second Language Writing* 1:109–22.

Johns, A. M. 1990. L1 composition theories: Implications for developing theories of L2 composition. In *Second language writing: Research insights for the classroom,* ed. B. Kroll, 24–36. Cambridge: Cambridge University Press.

———. 1995. Genre and pedagogical purposes. *Journal of Second Language Writing* 4:181–90.

———. 1997. *Text, role, and context.* Cambridge: Cambridge University Press.

Kaplan, R. B. 1966. Cultural thought patterns in inter-cultural education. *Language Learning* 16:1–20.

Kastorf, J. 1993. Robo teacher. *Sacramento Bee,* May 26, p. F6.

Kepner, C. G. 1991. An experiment in the relationship of types of written feedback to the development of second-language writing skills. *Modern Language Journal* 75:305–13.

Komura, K. 1999. Student response to error correction in ESL classrooms. Master's thesis, California State University, Sacramento.

Krashen, S. D. 1984. *Writing: Research, theory, and application.* Oxford: Pergamon Press.

Lalande, J. F., II. 1982. Reducing composition errors: An experiment. *Modern Language Journal* 66:140–49.

Lane, J., and E. Lange. 1999. *Writing clearly: An editing guide.* 2d ed. Boston: Heinle and Heinle.

Leki, I. 1990. Coaching from the margins: Issues in written response. In *Second language writing: Research insights for the classroom,* ed. B. Kroll, 57–68. Cambridge: Cambridge University Press.

———. 1991. The preferences of ESL students for error correction in college-level writing classes. *Foreign Language Annals* 24:203–18.

Messerschmitt, D. 1998. MA TESOL graduates' grammar weaknesses: Employers' perspectives. Paper presented at the CATESOL State Conference, April, Pasadena, Calif.

Nelson, G. L., and J. G. Carson. 1998. ESL students' perceptions of effectiveness in peer response groups. *Journal of Second Language Writing* 7:113–32.

Patthey-Chavez, G. G., and D. R. Ferris. 1997. Writing conferences and the weaving of multi-voiced texts in college composition. *Research in the Teaching of English* 31:51–90.

Peterson, J., and S. A. Hagen. 1999. *Better writing through editing.* Boston: McGraw-Hill.

Polio, C., C. Fleck, and N. Leder. 1998. "If only I had more time": ESL learners' changes in linguistic accuracy on essay revisions. *Journal of Second Language Writing* 7:43–68.

Radecki, P., and J. Swales. 1988. ESL student reaction to written comments on their written work. *System* 16:355–65.

Raimes, A. 1991. Out of the woods: Emerging traditions in teaching writing. *TESOL Quarterly* 25:407–30.

———. 1992. *Grammar troublespots.* New York: St. Martin's Press.

Reid, J. 1994. Responding to ESL students' texts: The myths of appropriation. *TESOL Quarterly* 28:273–92.

———. 1998a. "Eye" learners and "ear" learners: Identifying the language needs of international students and U.S. resident writers. In *Grammar in the composition classroom: Essays on teaching ESL for college-bound students,* by P. Byrd and J. M. Reid, 3–17. Boston: Heinle and Heinle.

———. 1998b. Responding to ESL student language problems: Error analysis and revision plans. In *Grammar in the composition classroom: Essays on teaching ESL for college-bound students,* by P. Byrd and J. M. Reid, 118–37. Boston: Heinle and Heinle.

Rennie, C. 2000. Error feedback in ESL writing classes: What do students really want? Master's thesis, California State University, Sacramento.

Robb, T., S. Ross, and I. Shortreed. 1986. Salience of feedback on error and its effect on EFL writing quality. *TESOL Quarterly* 20:83–93.

Roberts, B. J. 1999. Can error logs raise more than consciousness? The effects of error logs and grammar feedback on ESL students' final drafts. Master's thesis, California State University, Sacramento.

Santos, T. 1988. Professors' reactions to the academic writing of nonnative-speaking students. *TESOL Quarterly* 22:69–90.

Scarcella, R. 1996. Secondary education in California and second language research: Instructing ESL students in the 1990s. *CATESOL Journal* 9 (1): 129–52.

Schleppegrell, M. 1998. Grammar as resource: Writing a description. *Research in the Teaching of English* 32:182–211.

Schwartz, B. 1993. On explicit and negative data effecting and affecting competence and linguistic behavior. *Studies in Second Language Acquisition* 15:147–63.

Semke, H. 1984. The effects of the red pen. *Foreign Language Annals* 17:195–202.

Sheppard, K. 1992. Two feedback types: Do they make a difference? *RELC Journal* 23:103–10.

Silva, T. 1988. Comments on Vivian Zamel's "Recent research on writing pedagogy." *TESOL Quarterly* 22:517–19.

———. 1990. Second language composition instruction: Developments, issues, and directions in ESL. In *Second language writing: Research insights for the classroom,* ed. B. Kroll, 11–23. Cambridge: Cambridge University Press.

———. 1993. Toward an understanding of the distinct nature of L2 writing: The ESL research and its implications. *TESOL Quarterly* 27:657–77.

Silva, T., C. Brice, and M. Reichelt. 1999. *Annotated bibliography of scholarship in second language writing: 1993–1997.* Stamford, Conn.: Ablex.

Sommers, N. 1982. Responding to student writing. *College Composition and Communication* 33:148–56.

Spack, R. 1988. Initiating ESL students into the academic discourse community: How far should we go? *TESOL Quarterly* 22:29–51.

Straub, R. 1997. Students' reactions to teacher comments: An exploratory study. *Research in the Teaching of English* 31:91–119.

Swales, J. 1990. *Genre analysis: English in academic and research settings.* New York: Cambridge University Press.

Tannacito, D. 1995. *A guide to writing in English as a second or foreign language: An annotated bibliography of research and pedagogy.* Alexandria, Va.: TESOL.

Truscott, J. 1996. The case against grammar correction in L2 writing classes. *Language Learning* 46:327–69.

———. 1999. The case for "the case for grammar correction in L2 writing classes": A response to Ferris. *Journal of Second Language Writing* 8:111–22.

Vann, R., F. Lorenz, and D. Meyer. 1991. Error gravity: Faculty response to errors in written discourse of nonnative speakers of English. In *Assessing second language writing in academic contexts,* ed. L. Hamp-Lyons, 181–95. Norwood, N.J.: Ablex.

Vann, R., D. Meyer, and F. Lorenz. 1984. Error gravity: A study of faculty opinion of ESL errors. *TESOL Quarterly* 18:427–40.

VanPatten, B. 1988. How juries get hung: Problems with the evidence for a focus on form in teaching. *Language Learning* 38:243–60.

Weaver, C. 1996. *Teaching grammar in context.* Portsmouth, N.H.: Boynton/Cook Heinemann.

Zamel, V. 1982. Writing: The process of discovering meaning. *TESOL Quarterly* 16:195–209.

———. 1985. Responding to student writing. *TESOL Quarterly* 19:79–102.

———. 1987. Recent research on writing pedagogy. *TESOL Quarterly* 21:697–715.

Zhang, S. 1995. Reexamining the affective advantage of peer feedback in the ESL writing class. *Journal of Second Language Writing* 4:209–22.